B O A T I N G

WATERSPORTS

**The Ultimate Get-Started Guide
to Towing Fun**

Publisher/Book Division: Terrence Dorner

Written and Edited by: Jo Robertson

Research Editor: Susan Hash

Cover Photos by Tom King

Black and White Photography by Tom King

Cover and Interior Pages Designed by Meredith J. Rushing
& Associates Design

International Standard Book Number: 89-52016

Printed in U.S.A.

Notice: The publisher disclaims all liability in connection
with the use of this information. Always observe safe boating laws, utilize specialized protective flotation and skiing
equipment, and seek professional supervision before at-
tempting new skills.

D1295080

ACKNOWLEDGEMENTS

THANKS TO: A big thanks from *WaterSki* Magazine to all the folks who made this book possible, including Tony Klarich, Tony Finn, Mike Kjellander, Kent McMillan, Ron Scarpa, Britt and Tawn Larsen, Wally Sokolowski, and others who wrote the source books and articles used as references for this guide. Also, thanks to those skiers who provided their skills for the photos in this book: Donna Cox, Randy Meador, Brett Bainter, and Zack Meyers. They and others like them have contributed to the phenomenal growth of watersports in this country over the past few years.

SPECIAL THANKS TO: **O'Brien International**, manufacturers of a complete line of water skis and accessories. Call or write:

O'Brien International
14615 NE 91st Street
Redmond, Washington 98052
206-881-5900

MasterCraft, builders of a fine line of recreational and tournament ski boats, including the ProStar 190. Call or write:

MasterCraft Boat Company
Route 9, Box 152
Maryville, Tennessee 37801
615-983-2178

CONTENTS

BOATING WATERSPORTS

THE ULTIMATE GET-STARTED GUIDE TO TOWING FUN

C O N T E N T S   PAGE

INTRODUCTION

HERE'S ALL YOU NEED TO TOW

Is there anything more irresistible than the water?

Almost since birth, we are attracted to it and find it an exhilarating, refreshing medium, a buoyant playground supplying endless opportunities for recreation and relaxation. Over the last decade, boating and its related watersports have grown at a dizzying rate. And as more and more people are drawn to the water, they discover more and more ways to enjoy it.

INTRODUCTION

Whether you're a brand-new boat owner or a dedicated watersports enthusiast eager to expand your horizons, you're undoubtedly excited about all the towing options available today. But the whole watersports arena may be just a bit perplexing to you. After all, you may have seen boats towing skiers, kneeboarders, skiboarders, and tubers countless times, but do *you* know how to pull a skier, kneeboarder, skiboarder — or even a barefooter? Do you know how to ski, kneeboard, or skiboard yourself? Do you know what sort of equipment you need? Do you know the safety rules and regulations?

If you don't, never fear. The folks from *WaterSki* Magazine are ready to answer all your questions with this ultimate get-started guide.

WaterSki Magazine is the world's leading authority on watersports of every kind — from slalom skiing to kneeboarding to barefooting. Its publisher, writers, and editors have decades of experience in the field and an unparalleled knowledge of the industry.

What's more, *WaterSki* has a unique resource — the sport's leading experts. Skiers, coaches, industry reps, and technical wizards from every discipline have shared their invaluable expertise with the staff of the magazine.

O'Brien International is one of the world's largest manufacturers of high-quality water skis, kneeboards, skiboards, tubes — you name it. And now, *WaterSki* and O'Brien are pleased to share their experience and knowledge with you, the new boater and watersports enthusiast.

This book contains the fundamentals of skiing on a "combo" pair, slalom, hot dog slalom, kneeboarding, skiboarding, barefooting, trick skiing, tubing, and much more, gleaned from books and articles written for *WaterSki* by the experts in each discipline — all in one easy-to-follow format.

But now it's time to grab a cold one, settle into your seat, and get ready to learn all you need to tow!

CHAPTER 1

7

GO TOW IT

COMMON-SENSE RULES FOR WATERSPORTS

First things first: Watersports are wonderful, but playing on the water safely requires a healthy dose of caution and common sense. Here are some very basic rules to help make your days on the waterways both pleasant and risk-free.

▲ **Always wear a personal flotation device (PFD)** while water skiing, kneeboarding, and skiboarding. Choose a secure, durable lifejacket that allows for free movement; it shouldn't be bulky or awkward-feeling. A PFD will help you remain afloat even if you take a hard fall, and will also protect your ribcage and kidney areas. Also, you must carry a Coast Guard-approved PFD for every person on board your boat.

▲ **Insist on having a competent observer aboard** whenever you use your boat for skiing to communicate the skier's signals or status to the boat driver. The observer should also be able to assist the water skier physically if necessary. For this reason, it's a good idea that the observer be an adult or older teenager. In some states only a rearview mirror is required by law, but using an observer is always a wise precaution, even in boats equipped with mirrors.

▲ **Use established hand and verbal signals** familiar to the skier, towboat driver, and observer. Most verbal commands are used while preparing to ski. When you have your skis on and are ready for the driver to idle away slowly, say, "In gear," or "Take up slack." Never use "okay" or "ready"; the driver may accelerate before you are prepared.

When you're ready to go, shout, "Hit it!" If you're having trouble, say, "Neutral." Don't use "Hold it," which can sound like "Hit it," or "No," which sounds like "Go."

Once up and skiing, "thumbs up" means to go faster, "thumbs down" means to slow down, and the "okay" signal, with the thumb and forefinger forming an "O," means the speed is fine.

To turn, hold your arm vertical to the water, extend your forefinger, make a circling motion, then point in a wide arc to the right or left. The driver and observer can use these very same signals to tell you the boat will be turning.

To have the boat stop, do just what a traffic policeman would do to stop traffic; hold your arm up with the elbow at a 90-degree angle to the water and the palm facing forward. To return to the starting point, or to notify the driver and observer that you wish to end your session and get into the boat after a fall, pat your head.

To have the driver turn the boat's engine off, draw an index finger across your windpipe — just like a movie director does when he yells, "Cut!"

After each fall, it's important that you let the driver and observer know you're okay. To do so, clasp your hands over your head. Without that signal, the boat driver and observer must assume you're hurt and rush back to assist you. When you fall in a busy waterway, hold one of your skis at least half its length out of the water and even wave it back and forth to alert other boaters to your presence.

▲ **The skier must make sure that the towrope is straight and taut before giving the "Hit it" signal.** Confusion about the proper time to accelerate the boat could have serious consequences.

▲ **Give novice skiers lots of extra attention.** Initial ski rides (depending on the size and age of the skier) should be taken at speeds as slow as nine mph and should seldom, if ever, exceed 22 mph. Extra caution, gradual speed changes, and wide turns are essential to ensure an enjoyable ride for most novice skiers.

▲ **The driver and all passengers should be safely seated** when the boat is in motion, not standing or balanced against the gunnel or seat backrests.

▲ **The towboat driver must respond to the needs and requests of the skier** by maintaining an appropriate speed and direction. Under no circumstances should the boat driver and skier both start cutting back and forth in a contest to determine who is more skillful. This type of maneuver is very dangerous for the skier, as well as for the boat passengers and other waterway users.

▲ **Be a courteous and safety-conscious towboat driver** by maintaining a safe distance from other water activities, such as swimming, scuba diving, sailing, and fishing. Also, avoid driving in close proximity to the shore, stationary objects, narrow channels and harbors, and in any intensive use areas. Be sure to start skiing at a reasonable hour in the morning — be mindful of the rights of others.

▲ **Attempt to fall backwards or sideways** when skiing if a fall is inevitable.

▲ **Always become familiar with the waterway** on which you'll be boating and skiing. Striking an underwater object can be equally destructive to the boat and the water skier. Always ensure that there is a minimum water depth of four to five feet in the skiing area for water skiing, kneeboarding, or skiboarding, and five to six feet for barefooting.

▲ **Never drive a boat directly behind a water skier**, and always discourage other boats from doing the same. A tragedy could easily occur if a skier should suddenly fall in the path of a following boat.

▲ **The boat's motor should never be operating when a skier is boarding from the water.** Boat propellers sometimes rotate, even when the motor is in neutral. Disaster could strike if the shift lever inadvertently engages while the motor is running.

▲ **Don't ski directly toward a dock or a beach.** Any error in judgment could result in an injury. To end a ski ride, it's best to have the skier come to a stop within the boat's wake, while the boat is driven on a path that is parallel to the dock or beach. Then the skier should swim to shore or board the boat.

▲ **Don't antagonize other waterway users** by skiing nearby, turning to spray them in the process. This not only projects a poor image of water skiing to the non-skiing public, but could be dangerous if you make an error in judgment.

▲ **Never wrap the rope around any part of your body,** or place the handle behind your neck or knees, or place your arms or legs through the bridle. To fall in such a position carries the risk of serious injury.

▲ **Passengers should never pull the rope into the boat** while a skier is being towed. If the passenger loses his grip on the rope, a coil of the loose rope could cause injury to the skier or boat occupants.

WATERSPORTS

▲ **Replace or repair worn ropes, bridles, handles, or towrope attachment hardware** before they fail in service. An unexpected failure of any one of these towline components could injure an unsuspecting skier.

▲ **Avoid trailing the ski rope behind the boat** at high speeds and retrieve the rope as soon as the run is finished. If you fail to do either, the rope can be very hazardous to skiers, swimmers, and boat occupants.

▲ **Don't use extremely tight and unyielding water ski bindings**, which could cause injury in the case of a fall, since they may not allow the feet to be released. Some modern bindings with high boots and double wraps approach the security of a snow ski boot, but they lack the safety benefit of a secondary release mechanism. Such bindings are for experts only.

▲ **When trick skiing, use a trick release device** with a competent operator if toehold tricks and similar maneuvers are attempted. Without this equipment, a fall on even simple maneuvers could cause injury.

▲ **Stop boating and water skiing as soon as an electrical storm appears in the area.**

▲ **Prepare for the skiing season by keeping fit.** Try to condition all the active muscle groups to reduce early-season discomfort and the risk of injury. Also, stretch and warm up before you go skiing, kneeboarding, skiboarding, etc.

▲ **Never ski to a state of exhaustion**, since this unnecessarily increases the potential for injury.

▲ **Avoid making quick movements** when returning to a fallen skier if there are passengers riding in the bow section of a bowrider; they might be flung out of the boat. Also, the additional weight on the bow might alter the boat's handling and wake characteristics.

▲ **Protect yourself from hypothermia** when skiing during cool weather by wearing a wetsuit or drysuit for safety and comfort. Even in relatively warm water, your body temperature can drop to a dangerously low level if you remain in the water for an extended period of time.

▲ **Minimize the risk of injury by wearing a substantial bathing suit**, or better still, jump pants, a wetsuit, or cutoff jeans, when skiing at speeds higher than 25 mph (40 kph).

▲ **Use ropes of the same length** when towing two skiers behind a boat to avoid the possibility of one skier's falling in front of the other.

Also, use towropes made specifically for water skiing — they're strong, durable, and they float.

GO TOW IT

GEARING UP

Behind-the-boat tubing has been popular since the truck tire was invented. If you like your equipment clean and blissfully free of tar and oil, however, the new tubes on the market should suit you just fine. The old-fashioned innertube has become an exciting form of water recreation — with performance not found in most tubes and durability to boot. Some tubes even have handles to aid control.

There's not a whole lot of equipment needed for tow-tubing, but a couple of items are *de rigeur*. First, your boat must be equipped with either a tow pylon or a rear towing eye, and all tubers, young and old, must don a personal flotation device (PFD). The tube should be attached directly to the boat, so no ropes or handles are needed.

Once you've got your gear together, you're ready to go tubing.

WATERSPORTS

TUBE TIME

No matter how serious you are about learning to ski, there's still a time for having fun. And having fun means everything from being silly to getting a thrill to just enjoying yourself while learning new skills. Most of all, since your boat may be your prime recreational outlet, play time means getting towed.

For many people, the weekdays are for dreaming about the weekends. Perhaps you fantasize about how you can eke out one more bit of pleasure from your powerboat. If you're willing to try anything, you've got plenty to choose from, because water toys are everywhere these days.

Tubing is probably the simplest form of towing, so it's a great place to start. You don't need any special athletic abilities to sit in a tube behind the boat; all you need is the right equipment, some basic knowledge, and a healthy regard for safety.

So come along, tow your wild oats, and get in the mood for tubing.

TOW TUBING

PHOTO ONE

Once the tube is inflated attach a towrope that's up to 75 feet long to the towing harness on the front of the tube, if there is one, or wrap the rope securely around the tube. Have the tube rider put on a PFD and sit in the tube, grasping the handles. The rider can begin either on the beach or on the water.

PHOTO TWO

Once the rider yells, "Hit it!" the driver should accelerate slowly up to speed. Never exceed 25 mph when towing adults or 15 mph when towing children.

WATERSPORTS

CONCEPTS AND COMMENTS

Tow-tubing is one of the most basic of towing activities, yet it can't be done haphazardly, particularly when children are involved. Be sure to use good common sense and to have an observer on board the towboat to keep an eye on the tuber and communicate with the driver.

DRIVING FOR TUBERS

One of the most exciting boat-driving patterns when pulling a tube is a wide, arcing "S" pattern. This puts the tube into a slight "whip," carrying it wide outside the boat wake. As the driver arcs the boat in the opposite direction, the tube hits the wake and gives the rider an exciting, "bouncy" ride to the other side.

Take care not to whip the tuber too fast or too hard!

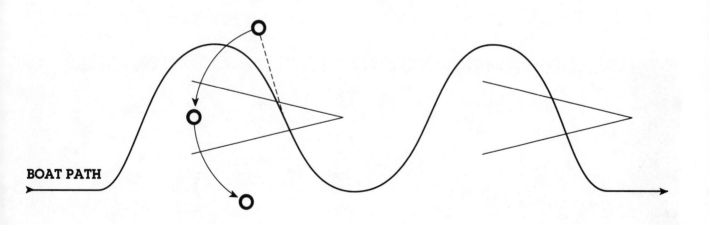

BOAT PATH

CHAPTER 2:
STARTING OUT ON COMBOS

GET READY TO SKI ON TWO

If you're looking for a cool change, nothing beats the exhilaration of water skiing. Young and old alike can enjoy the pleasure of skimming over the water's surface with the wind in their faces and spectacular walls of spray at their backs.

Over 18 million Americans water ski. Some are die-hard competitive skiers who are every bit as talented as athletes in such popular sports as football and basketball, but most are recreational skiers who head to the water for some dynamic relaxation.

Because it's relatively easy to learn to ski with the proper equipment and instruction, water skiing is a sport the whole family can enjoy. Once you get started, you may find yourself devoting whole weekends to skiing and inviting friends along to share the excitement.

The first step in becoming a true water skier is to learn to "ski on two," or a "combo pair." Once you get the hang of it, you'll be hooked for life!

WATERSPORTS

GEARING UP

All you really need to start "skiing on two" are a pair of combo skis, a personal flotation device (PFD), a towboat, and a towrope. You've already read everything you need to know about PFDs and towropes in the first chapter, so let's concentrate on your skis.

Combos are essentially beginners' skis, and thus should be very stable and forgiving. They generally are built to track straight and turn easily, but they are by no means inferior; some feature the sort of craftsmanship usually found in more advanced slalom skis. You can certainly learn to ski on a pair of combos you've picked up at a garage sale or rescued from a friend's basement, but you'll make the learning process much easier by acquiring a new pair that makes use of all the advancements in ski technology that have come about over the last several years.

To get the skis that are best for you — and your entire family, if you plan to share skis — it's best to visit your local ski shop and get individual attention. The salesperson will be able to help you select the pair that is just right for your height, weight, and athletic ability.

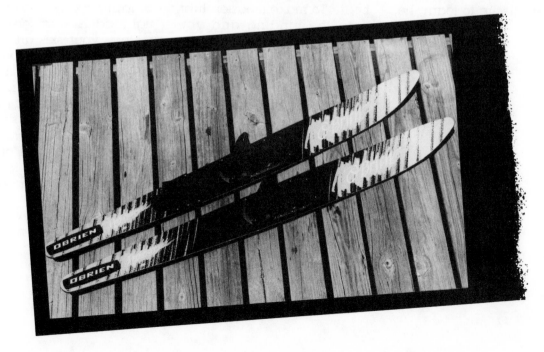

Incidentally, if you plan to teach small children to ski, you may want to check on special trainer skis. Trainers consist of a set of small skis that are tied together. The towrope is attached directly to the front crosstie of the skis, so that the child need only stand in place. The entire assembly is towed like a sled. Even toddlers can be taught to ski without the use of a boat; the adult simply pulls the child by hand along a beach. It's up to the family involved to determine when a child is ready to learn to ski, of course, but generally speaking, when a child is old enough to ask and expresses a sincere desire to learn, he's all set.

GETTING INTO YOUR SKIS

Ironically, just putting on a pair of skis can be one of the most difficult aspects of skiing! If you learn how to do it properly, however, you'll enjoy your first skiing experience all the more.

It's also important to learn how to control your skis once you're in the water. Many novices are so exasperated and exhausted after wrestling with the skis that there's no way they could ever pull off a successful start.

First, make sure your bindings are adjusted properly. Check the fit by putting on your skis on the dock or in the boat. To make it easier, lubricate the binding and your foot thoroughly before putting on a ski with water, liquid dishwashing detergent (no kidding), or a special binding lubricant. If you adjust the bindings when dry, they'll feel loose in the water.

To put a ski on, bend the heel piece of the binding over to one side and force your foot into the toe piece as far as it will go. Next, using both hands, grip the top of the heel piece and pull up while pushing your heel down flat against the ski, like pulling on a boot. If you have trouble putting the ski on, chances are good that your foot is not far enough into the toe piece.

The bindings should be snug but comfortable. You should be able to lift each ski without feeling as if it's going to come off, but the bindings should not pinch or be uncomfortably tight. If either binding is too loose or too tight, adjust it accordingly.

Once your skis are on and the bindings have been adjusted, put on your ski vest and get in the water.

Sooner or later you're going to have to put your skis on in the water. The technique is similar to that used on land, of course, but it's trickier because you don't have anything solid to push against. After awhile, however, it will become second nature to you.

First, bend the heel piece over with one hand as you did on land, but this time hold it there by grasping the edge of the ski. Grasp the toe piece with your other hand. Sink the ski beneath you and insert your foot in the toe piece as far as you can. Next, pull up sharply on the heel piece with both hands while plunging your heel down against the ski. If this is done in one quick motion, the water will provide enough resistance to push against, and the foot will slip into place.

Keep your foot at right angles and push with your leg. Try to keep the ski beneath you; don't let it float to the surface. Hunch your upper body forward to keep the ski under water. If necessary, take a breath and put your face in the water.

When you have the first ski on, draw your leg up close to your chest. Now, put the other ski on in the same manner. With both hands occupied and one ski already on, you will probably roll out of position. Regain your balance before sinking the second ski; work quickly and use the ski that's already on as an underwater stabilizer.

It will feel strange at first to have both skis on. You can't kick, and because skis are buoyant by design, they'll try to float you out of position. Keep your body in a compact ball and stay on top of your bindings by hunching forward. Stabilize yourself by using your arms to tread water.

If you lose control and can't maintain your body position, don't panic. Recover by floating on your side and drawing your knees up toward your chest, bringing the skis together again slowly. From here you can sink the skis and use your arms to rotate into an upright position. Relax and move slowly. Flow into position rather than trying to fight it.

Practice until you have the knack of putting on the skis and maintaining control of them. When you first learn to water ski you'll have to put your skis on again and again, so spend all the extra time you need to gain confidence.

TWO-SKI BODY POSITION

Do not ski bent forward at the waist. Instead, keep your head up and straighten your back and shoulders. This will help you maintain control over your skis and you'll be able to ski longer with less fatigue.

Lower your hips, tilt them back slightly, and keep your knees bent. Remember to face the boat or horizon. If you look down, you'll fall down, because the body almost always follows the head.

WATERSPORTS

Bring your skis close together, and lower the rope handle slightly. Your arms can be extended, but they must be relaxed. Grasp the handle in the baseball grip, with one palm down and one palm up. This is will give you additional strength. You can also use the palms-down grip if you prefer.

This is the proper water skiing position — with the head up, back erect, knees bent, and eyes on the horizon. No matter how serious or casual you are about your skiing, using this fundamental position of strength will allow you to advance your skills and improve in all areas of the sport.

CONCEPTS AND COMMENTS

Most beginners feel pretty wobbly when they first get up, and it takes time to develop stability. Nonetheless, you'll do yourself a big favor by concentrating on using the proper form even when you're just starting out. Later on, you'll be glad you started off right and developed good skiing habits — your lower back and arms will thank you, too!

DEEPWATER START

PHOTO ONE

Once you're out in the water, orient yourself so that you're facing the towboat. Have the driver idle slowly out from you to pull the rope taut. The correct position for a two-ski deepwater start is similar to that for doing a "cannonball" jump into a swimming pool. Draw your knees to your chest and hunch your shoulders forward against them.

Keep the skis parallel to one another and hold them close together, not quite touching, with the tips extending just a bit above the water. Your arms should be outstretched on either side of your knees. Hold the handle at the ends, not in the center, using the "baseball grip"; that is, one hand should be palm up, the other palm down. (The palms-down grip is also appropriate.)

WATERSPORTS

PHOTO TWO

When all the slack has been taken out of the rope and you're ready, tell the driver to "Hit it." Hold the handle low as the boat accelerates strongly but smoothly to about 18 mph — less for smaller skiers or children. Don't pull on the rope; simply resist the pull from the boat. Look ahead at the boat or at the horizon, not down at your skis. (If you look down, you'll fall down.) Freeze in the cannonball position and let the boat pull you up. Stay crouched once you're on top of the water, and don't start to stand until you feel steady.

PHOTO THREE

Once you feel sure of yourself and your skis are under complete control, slowly rise to the skiing position, with your back and head erect, arms straight, knees well bent, and skis close together. Don't bend your arms and pull forward! You will crash out the front. Don't try to stand up too quickly! You will put too much slack in the rope. Keep your arms straight and hold them to the sides of your body, so that you can lean against the pull of the boat and use it for leverage to help you get up.

TROUBLESHOOTING

Problem: Pulling on the tow-rope.

Solution: Most beginners instinctively pull on the rope when the boat begins to accelerate, which usually causes them to fall. Fight the instinct to pull on the rope. Instead, use it to steer from side to side.

Problem: Standing up too soon.

Solution: It is also natural to want to stand as soon as the boat accelerates. Once you get out of the cannonball position, however, you become top-heavy and will fall over. Your skis will also have a tendency to spread apart. Stay down on your heels until well after you are up and skiing in good control. Don't be in a hurry to stand up. You can continue to ski in a squat on your entire first attempt, if necessary.

Problem: Losing your balance.

Solution: To maintain your balance, it's important to keep your weight centered over your skis. Keep the skis pointed straight ahead or use the tension on the rope to help maintain balance.

Problem: Failure to keep the skis close together.

Solution: When the skis "split apart" on takeoff, you've probably tried to stand up too soon. If you stay crouched, your skis will stay together. Keep the skis parallel and just slightly apart.

CONCEPTS AND COMMENTS

Contrary to popular belief, you don't have to struggle to get up on a pair of water skis. If you stay crouched in the cannonball position, your start will be almost effortless, because the boat will do all the work. All you have to do is stay balanced.

If you go limp when the boat accelerates, you'll be pulled forward out the front, so brace yourself to stay over your bindings. This does *not* mean leaning back or pulling on the rope, because this will cause you to fall backward. Just keep your ankles, legs, back, and shoulders rigid to stay in the cannonball position and resist the pull on the rope as the boat moves forward.

To keep your balance, hold your skis together and steer by moving the rope from one side to the other as needed. It will take only a slight movement to compensate for any lack of balance. If you begin to tilt to one side, shift the handle in that direction a few inches to counteract the lean and maintain your equilibrium. Remember, however, not to pull on the rope.

WATERSPORTS

SITTING DOCK START

PHOTO ONE

Put your skis on and sit on the edge of the dock. Coil the towrope neatly and place the coils in the water in front of you. (Do not pay out the rope by hand.) Tell the driver to idle forward.

PHOTO TWO

As the last coil of rope is pulled tight, shift your weight from the dock to the skis. Crouch down and hold the handle in close so that you don't get pulled too far forward.

PHOTO THREE

When the rope is taut, tell the driver to "Hit it!" As the boat accelerates, you'll be pulled into the water. Keep your weight back a bit on your skis, and crouch low. Your body should be in a position similar to the one you assume in a deepwater start.

PHOTO FOUR

Once you feel steady and comfortable, gradually rise to the standing position. Remember to resist the pull of the boat, but not to pull on the rope.

TROUBLESHOOTING

Problem: Getting pulled out the front.
Solution: Don't give the boat too much rope. If you do, the boat will be traveling too fast when the rope tightens, and you'll get pulled over your ski tips. Also, ask the driver to accelerate more slowly.

Problem: Handle pops out of your hands.
Solution: Again, have the driver acclerate more slowly.

Problem: Sinking on takeoff.
Solution: If you allow too little rope to pay out before telling the driver to go, the boat may not be traveling fast enough and you'll sink as soon as you leave the dock. It may take several tries to get the timing exactly right.

CONCEPTS AND COMMENTS

You'll feel a more sudden pull on the rope in a sitting dock start than in a deepwater start, but if you're fairly accomplished with the latter, you shouldn't have much trouble.

There are a few important considerations, however. First, the dock should be just high enough off the water that your ankles are at water level when you're sitting on the edge. The water beneath the dock should also be fairly deep — at least six feet — so that you don't risk spinal cord injury in a hard fall. The dock surface where you sit should be free of splinters, cleats, nails, posts, hooks, or other protrusions that could snag your towrope or swimsuit — a dangerous and potentially embarrassing proposition!

Never ever attempt the sitting dock start unless you have an experienced driver, an alert observer, and the proper dock and water conditions, as just outlined.

STEERING AND WAKE CROSSING

PHOTO ONE

To change direction on a pair of skis, start skiing in a stable, controlled position. Then rotate your skis and tilt your shoulders in the direction you wish to travel. Lean back. This puts your skis on edge (on their sides) to slice through the water. The more you lean and the sharper the skis are angled, the faster you will cut to the side.

PHOTO TWO

Bend your knees and pull in and down slightly on the handle. Practice weaving back and forth within the wake and get used to the way your skis feel. Be sure to keep the skis close together and parallel when turning.

PHOTO THREE

Once you feel confident and in control, try crossing the boat wake. Think of the wake as a continuous wave moving along the surface of the water. Since the boat creates the wake at the same time it tows you, you'll be moving at the same speed as the wake. Start edging toward the wake with your skis at an angle. Do not attempt to cross the wake head on or with your skis held exactly parallel to the wake.

Keep your skis on edge all the way up and over the wake to maintain your momentum, and cross the crest at an angle. Continue to pull hard and lean until both skis have crossed the crest (the peak of the wake). Keep your skis close together, or you may get hung up on the crest.

TROUBLESHOOTING

Problem: Wake is too large, turbulent, or has a double crest.

Solution: Try crossing the wake at a slightly higher boat speed. Also, if you have an outboard boat, experiment with different tilt settings. Redistribute the weight in the boat to make sure it's balanced and remove any extra gear to create a more consistent wake.

Problem: Sliding back down in the middle of the wake.

Solution: Keep your skis on edge and maintain speed. If you try to cross the wake too slowly or with your skis held parallel, you'll have no chance of success.

CONCEPTS AND COMMENTS

Skiing inside the wake directly behind the boat is fun, but it can't compare with the exhilaration you'll experience skiing outside the wake. Once you've learned to cross the wake, you can start cutting harder by leaning and pulling. When you stop pulling, you drift back in toward the wake. As a result, it is easier to cross the wake from the outside heading in, but it's still important to cross the crest at an angle and with your skis together. When skiing in the rough water or rollers from other boats that are typically found outside the wake, just flex your knees more to cushion the ride.

LENDING A
HELPING HAND

Once you've learned to ski, you'll undoubtedly want to teach your friends or members of your family to ski, too — if only to have some experienced assistance on the water. After all, skiing is certainly not a solitary activity; it takes at least a trio of skier, driver, and observer.

Unfortunately, teaching another person to ski is some-

thing that is usually done haphazardly at best. Too often, a novice at a lakeside party is thrown a pair of skis, told to strap them on, gets two or three tries, and is then unceremoniously dumped back on shore while the "experts" ski to their heart's content.

There is a better way.

First, remember that new experiences are often frightening to people, even adults. Skiing may seem like a perfectly simple activity, once you've got the hang of it, but a beginner may be very apprehensive and confused. For this reason, it's best to start in a secluded cove or quiet area and focus entirely on the beginner's training.

Here are a few other tips:

▲ Go over all the safety rules of skiing with the new skier and make sure he or she has a firm understanding of all hand signals.

▲ Start in water that's comfortably deep, but not over the new skier's head.

▲ Use a shorter towrope; you may want to take some line off the usual 75-foot rope or use a special training bridle.

▲ A newer innovation in ski-related equipment is the barefoot boom. Designed to help beginning barefoot skiers, it is also a wonderful training device for new combo skiers or children because it allows them to begin right next to the ski boat where the trainer can give instructions. If you have access to a boom, use it.

▲ Help the skier get into the bindings and explain the basic body position for the start. Remind the beginner to resist the pull of the boat rather than pulling on the rope and emphasize that it's not necessary to struggle to get up.

▲ Assist the skier as he or she assumes the cannonball position and help align the skis properly in the water.

▲ Remind the skier that it's not necessary to get up quickly once the boat accelerates; it's fine to stay crouched in the cannonball position halfway around the lake, if need be.

▲ Beware of hypothermia — a serious drop in body temperature. While most waterways may seem perfectly warm at first, spending an hour or two in even 70-degree water can lower the body's temperature to life-threatening levels. Young children are particularly susceptible to hypothermia. Don't overdo it.

▲ Fatigue is another factor. Practice may make perfect, but it can also tire out even the most stalwart of skiers. A tired enthusiast won't remain enthusiastic for long — and won't be a successful new skier.

▲ Above all, be patient with the new skier. A lucky few will be able to ski on their very first tries, but most people require several attempts and a lot of encouragement. Be prepared to teach the initiate at his or her own pace.

SKIING ON ONE: A SINGULAR SENSATION

THE THRILL OF SLALOM

Once you feel comfortable and relaxed turning and cutting on combos, you'll long for the joys of slalom — or, more accurately, skiing on one. By dropping one of your skis, you'll gain significant leverage against the boat and you can attain a much greater skiing angle. As a result, you'll cross the wake faster, make better, more controlled turns, and kick up some pretty spectacular walls of spray.

The professional side of water skiing is made up of three events: tricks (which we cover in a later chapter), jumping (which is taught strictly through personal, pro-fessional instruction), and slalom (the most beautiful of the three to watch). In slalom-course skiing, the skier takes on six red buoys, speeding across the wakes and whipping around each one, at progressively shorter and shorter line lengths. It takes skill, finesse, and a whole lot of determination.

Recreational slalom, or "open-water" slalom, is a good deal less demanding, but every bit as much fun. And fun is what water skiing's all about. So now it's time to drop one ski and enjoy the thrill of a singular sensation!

WATERSPORTS

GEARING UP

If you glance at your combo skis, you'll notice that one comes equipped with both a front and rear binding. This ski is designed so that once you progress, you can drop the other member of the pair and slalom on it. Now, this is certainly a good way to learn to ski on one, but you'll very quickly want to acquire a ski made especially for slalom, rather than continuing on the combo ski.

Buying a slalom ski is not always an easy task. It's important to cut through the flashy graphics and bright colors to find the ski that's best for you. For this reason, it's a good idea to visit a ski shop to let the sales professionals find the ski that best meets your needs.

As a new slalom skier, you'll want to choose a ski that's stable and makes getting up and turning an easy proposition. Certain skis are designed specifically for the entry-level enthusiast, but that doesn't mean they're inferior in any way. Today's skis are incredibly advanced over the old wooden planks of yesteryear and have certain design characteristics that are worth knowing a little something about.

The overall performance of any given ski is determined by a number of design features that complement one another. For example, the way the edge of the ski is shaped, the overall profile of the ski, and the width of its tail all help determine how deeply it will ride in the water and how easily it will make a deep-water start.

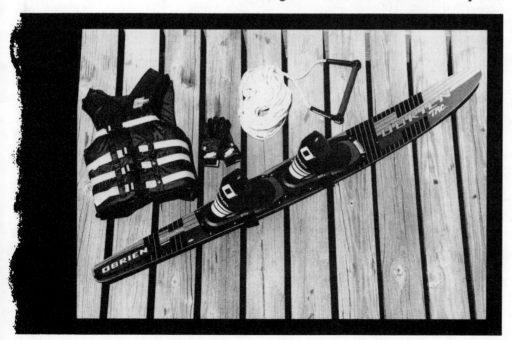

Other variables are the flexibility of the ski, both overall and in certain key areas, its responsiveness, and the shape of its fin, which is located on the underside of the ski. All are important factors in a ski's performance, but no one factor determines how a ski will perform for you. Your height, weight, and level of athletic ability are all important considerations.

Happily, entry-level slaloms are somewhat less expensive than their high-performance counterparts, and you'll certainly want to choose a beginner's model when you're just starting out. At this stage of your development, you simply won't have the necessary control over high-end skis to make them perform for you. Entry-level skis feature adjustable bindings to suit a wide variety of skiers and crisply beveled edges to help the ski attain and hold an angle. They are softer, more forgiving, and handle well at slower speeds. What's more, beginners' skis don't generate excessive speed because softer skis give in to the force of the pull rather than resisting it. All in all, they provide the novice with much greater control to make skiing all the more fun and rewarding.

As always, you'll want to wear your comfortable, properly fitting ski vest, gloves, and perhaps a wetsuit if you've got one, and employ all the rules of water skiing safety.

BOAT DRIVING TIP
The following chart will help you select the best ski size for you and your proper slalom speed.

SIZE/WEIGHT MANEUVER CHART		
WEIGHT (LBS)	**SKI SIZE**	**SPEED**
100-120	65"	28
120-140	65"	30
140-160	65" or 67"	31
160-180	67"	33
180-200	67" or 69"	35

WATERSPORTS

PUT YOUR BEST FOOT FORWARD

The first thing you must do when learning to "ski on one" is to figure out which foot you'll place forward on the ski and which you'll place in the rear binding. Don't worry: It's pretty easy to determine whether you should stand with your left foot forward (which is the more common of the two methods) or with your right foot forward (sometimes called the "goofy-foot" stance).

Incidentally, "goofy-foot" is in no way a derogatory term. As a matter of fact, many of the best skiers in the world ski with their right feet forward. Here are a few of the best ways to figure out which foot to place forward:

▲ Stand on a skateboard and roll slowly forward. You will naturally stand in the way that's better for you.

▲ Pretend that you are hitting a baseball. Generally speaking, if you hit the ball with your right foot forward, you will also be more comfortable skiing with your right foot forward.

▲ Kick a ball. Nine times out of 10, the foot that you naturally kick with will be your forward foot.

If you try all these experiments and get mixed results (which is very unlikely), just plan to ski with your left foot forward, as most people do. If it doesn't feel right, it takes only a few minutes to reverse skis and try again.

DEEPWATER START

PHOTO ONE

Float in the water and pull the ski leg knee into your chest, with your rear foot dragging behind your body. Be sure to have the ski tip at least four inches above the surface of the water. Keep your arms slightly bent. Right-foot-forward skiers should start with the ski on the right side of the rope and left-foot-forward skiers should start with the ski on the left.

PHOTO TWO

As the boat accelerates, resist the pull with your upper body and arms. Keep your chest over your knee to help the ski plane with minimal resistance. The ski's attitude should not be perpendicular to the water. Rather, it should be almost parallel to the surface. Drag your rear foot directly behind and use it as a rudder for stability.

PHOTO THREE

Keeping your head level and your arms straight, use your stomach muscles to steer the ski in a straight path. Begin standing up, and continue to keep your chest over your knee. Do not rush standing up.

PHOTO FOUR

After reaching the standing position, slowly place your rear foot in the binding. Do so by "feel" — not by looking down at the ski. When you're in the final slalom position, your weight should be evenly distributed over both feet, both knees should be bent, your hips should be pushed forward, and your arms should be straight.

TROUBLESHOOTING

Problem: Burying the ski tip and falling forward.

Solution: This happens when you don't keep the ski tip up or you lean too far forward. Push the ski tip farther above the surface and position your shoulders back farther to resist the boat's pull.

Problem: Ski plows through the water.

Solution: Caused by leaning away from the boat. This makes the ski plow in an angle perpendicular to the surface. Lean forward and push the ski into a planing position. Take care not to overcompensate and dig the ski tip.

Problem: Falling to the side.

Solution: Caused by allowing the ski to veer to the side. Maintain a straight path by flexing your stomach and leg muscles for directional stability. For those experiencing *extreme* difficulty, a double-handled rope may help keep the ski straight during take-off. After you become proficient, begin using a single handle again.

CONCEPTS AND COMMENTS

Starting with one foot in the binding is the very foundation of successful slalom skiing. When you advance, you will most likely want to progress to starting with two feet in the bindings.

BOAT DRIVING TIP

After the skier's rope is tight, put the boat in gear for one or two seconds before accelerating. This allows the ski to break a path with the ski and rise more parallel to the water's surface before take-off. Accelerate firmly and smoothly to normal slalom speed. Analyze each skier's needs to determine whether a fast, moderate, or slow start is best. For example, smaller or less experienced skiers usually require a slower start than larger, more advanced skiers.

WATERSPORTS

STEERING AND WAKE CROSSING

PHOTO ONE

As you learn to keep your weight centered over the ski, you'll gain confidence and develop balance and you'll be ready to steer. To turn, shift your weight to the back of the ski and bend your legs to absorb any "chatter" from the water.

PHOTO TWO

Tilt your shoulders in the direction you wish to travel and lean back. This puts your ski on edge to slice through the water. The more you lean and the sharper the ski is angled, the faster you will cut. Bend your knees and pull in and down slightly on the handle. Practice weaving back and forth within the wake and get used to the way your ski feels.

PHOTO THREE

Now it's time to cross the wake. Start edging toward it with your ski at an angle. Do not attempt to cross the wake head on or with your ski held parallel to it.

Keep your ski on edge all the way up and over the wake to maintain your momentum, and cross the crest at an angle. Continue to pull hard and lean until you've crossed the crest. To proceed outside the wake, lean against the pull of the boat toward the direction you want to go on the side or edge of the ski. You will have more balance while the ski is on edge rather than skiing flat or directly behind the boat. Always try to point the tip of the ski into the wake for smoother wake crossings.

TROUBLESHOOTING

Problem: Breaking forward at the waist when crossing the wakes.

Solution: Contrary to popular opinion, huge biceps, chest measurements, and forearm strength have very little to do with correct slalom technique. Used correctly, body strength is an asset, but slalom is really all about leverage — the optimum use of your body against the boat.

Hip position is the key here. Your hips allow your lower back to resist the boat, your back being your greatest asset. In the correct position, your lower back can handle an enormous pull from the towboat, and thereby increase your angle and acceleration. This will help keep you from breaking at the waist.

CONCEPTS AND COMMENTS

Slalom is an exciting event for both beginners and experts, and one of its most exhilarating aspects is the pull through the wakes. Done properly, you'll experience a sensation of speed and control.

It's crucial to pull properly in order to cross both wakes. Even longline skiers who are just learning to slalom must be able to "lean" properly through the wakes to gain the maximum amount of angle.

It's also important to flex your knees. In fact, your knees should *always* be bent — they are your body's built-in "shock absorbers." Bent knees are especially important for crossing the wakes because the wakes are hard and can easily throw you off balance. Try to push both your knees and ankles forward, because bending your ankles as well as your knees enables you to keep your rear-end tucked in.

Always keep your shoulders back; they resist the pull of the boat. The best way to keep your shoulders back is to push your hips forward and to bring the handle into your hip. When skiing in this position, the strain of the pull is absorbed by your body rather than your lower back. If you are feeling a lot of strain on your lower back, try pushing your shoulders farther back and your hips farther forward.

PERFECTING THE SLALOM PATTERN

You will become a much better skier and progress much more rapidly if you learn and understand the basics of the slalom pattern. Slalom water skiing is broken down into four major components: the preturn, the turn, the pull, and the edge change. When performed in the proper sequence and with good technique, in or out of the slalom course, these four elements will become one fluid, dynamic, exciting motion.

Here's how these four components fit together.

The **preturn** is the stage that takes place just after the edge change. It helps the ski decelerate and prepare for the turn as well as for a change in direction.

The **turn** is the point at which the skier changes direction. This is the phase that people most frequently associate with the sport of slalom skiing. It is at this point that the skier reaches the slowest point in the slalom pattern and it prepares him for the next stage. Not surprisingly, most falls take place during the turn.

The next stage is the **pull** or acceleration phase. The rope tightens and the skier enters into a tug-of-war with the boat in a race to cross the wakes quickly and execute another turn.

Immediately following the pull is the **edge change** — a quick but essential ingredient of proper slalom skiing. At this stage, the ski stops accelerating, then rolls from the outside edge to the inside edge, and begins to decelerate in preparation for the next preturn and turn.

This cycle repeats itself six times for tournament skiers who use a slalom course. For open-water skiers, the sequence can be repeated until the skier runs out of energy!

The most important tasks in slalom skiing are to maintain a smooth and fluid pattern and to emphasize proper technique and body positioning. If you concentrate on executing these two tasks, you will most certainly meet most of your slalom goals.

THE WAKES: YOUR PRIMARY REFERENCE POINT

Whether you ski in a slalom course or out in open water, use the wakes as your primary reference point to develop or enhance a smooth slalom rhythm. How long or short you pull should be thought of in relationship to the wake, as should your timing for changing edges. If you use the wake for a reference, you will have a foolproof guide for starting your preturn and turn. Everything keys off the wake.

Contrary to popular belief, many top slalom skiers use the wake, not the buoys, as their primary reference point, because the bump of the wake is a signal to the skier to begin changing edges and to start the turn. Usually, a top slalom skier hasn't even looked for the next buoy at this point; instead, he knows its position almost by instinct because he has used the wake as his primary point of reference. Only after completing the edge change does the avid slalomer search for the secondary point of reference — the buoy.

The rules for open-water skiers are the same, and these skiers will benefit greatly by using this reference system because it offers dependable, consistent, useful benchmarks. Also, the open-water skier does not have the benefit of the secondary reference point (the buoy) to guide him.

Here's a real life example of how the wakes are used as reference points. Assuming the skier has completed the first turn, he then pulls firmly to a point approximately five feet past the second wake before changing edges and making a turn. On the return, the skier must take care to pull exactly the same distance back across the wake, making sure to let up again just five feet past the wake. The edge change takes place and the slalom pattern continues.

A skier who employs the wake reference system will develop a rhythmic, smooth pattern with turns that look almost identical on both sides.

Avoid falling into a trap common to many skiers. They have an extremely bad side and a "just okay" opposite side, usually because they haven't made themselves aware that the wakes are their guides to improved performance.

CHAPTER 4:
HOT DOG! IT'S TIME TO SHOW OFF

DOGGING IT DOWN

Once you're comfortable maneuvering on one ski, you'll undoubtedly yearn to show off a little — or maybe a lot! If that's the case, then it's time to learn a few "hot dog" slalom moves that'll have the rest of your buddies playing catch-up!

Hot dog skiing is sometimes called freestyle, and if you've ever attended a professional tournament, the term "free-styler" may have you quaking in your bindings. Well, don't panic. The guys you see performing advanced maneuvers off the ramp are expert show skiers — they may look fearless, but they're really seasoned athletes. The moves you'll learn in this chapter can be accomplished by any slalom skier who maintains a healthy respect for safety and sanity.

When learning these maneuvers, make sure you master each step before you progress to the next one and limit your attempts to a few tries each set. Don't keep trying to accomplish a trick until you can't hold onto the rope anymore! Skiing your buns off is no way to become the top hot dog on your lake.

Work on one or two tricks at a time and stick with them until you perform them successfully about 95 percent of the time. Then go on to the next one.

Now it's time to *dog it down!*

GEARING UP Selecting the proper equipment is important if you want to learn tricks faster and avoid injuries. First, you'll need a slalom ski that's wider in the body and tail sections to help you jump higher and land more softly. Also, the ski should have a full hyperparabolic (rail-to-rail) tunnel, which makes it ride higher in the water, reduces drag, and lets the ski track straighter.

Look for a ski with a moderate to large degree of rocker, the curvature of the ski from front to back. A ski with greater rocker puts more of its surface area in contact with the wake during wake tricks, providing you with a better platform from which to make higher jumps with less effort. You may also want to remove the wing (also called a stabilizer or cheater) from the fin because it increases drag and keeps the ski in the water. Without it, you can jump higher and ski longer.

Wear a wetsuit, at least during the learning stages, to reduce the risk of injury to your legs and groin. A suit at least three millimeters thick with cinch straps at both legs to prevent water from rushing into the suit is recommended.

Always wear a snugly fitting Coast Guard-approved PFD, preferably a four-buckle vest for rib and stomach protection, and use a standard 75-foot rope. If you have gloves, wear them. They're not absolutely essential, but they'll give you a better grip and allow you to ski longer.

B O A T   D R I V I N G   T I P
Use this chart to determine your proper hot dog slalom speed.

Note: Test different ski sizes to suit your personal style. This chart should be used only as a general guideline.

SIZE/WEIGHT MANEUVER CHART		
WEIGHT (LBS)	**SKI SIZE**	**SPEED**
100-120	65"	28
120-140	65"	30
140-160	65" or 67"	31
160-180	67"	33
180-200	67" or 69"	35

SINGLE WAKE JUMP

PHOTO ONE

Begin your cut about 10 feet outside the wake and put the ski on edge by leaning away from the boat. Stop edging about five feet from the wake and flatten the ski to create more surface area for lift.

PHOTO TWO

Bend your knees slightly before hitting the wake. Concentrate on maintaining proper form (keep your head up and your shoulders square) as you extend your legs and pop straight up off the crest of the wake. The key to a good pop is to fully extend your legs.

PHOTO THREE

While in the air, it's important to keep your head up and your shoulders square. Hold the rope in near your waist with your arms slightly bent. DO NOT drop your head to look down, but spot the landing with your eyes.

PHOTO FOUR

Absorb the shock of the landing by bending your knees. Do not break forward at the waist or let your arms extend all the way out. You should land with your weight distributed evenly over your feet.

TROUBLESHOOTING

Problem: Can't get any height off the wake.

Solution: This is generally caused by timing the pop poorly. Your legs should reach their full extension as the mid-section of the ski reaches the crest of the wake. You may also have difficulty jumping high if you don't bend your knees enough. If you feel this might be your problem, bend your knees more.

Problem: Landing off-balance.

Solution: You may very well land off-balance if you don't pop straight up. Be sure not to pop off to the side. Concentrating on riding a "flat" ski into the wake helps keep your weight centered over the ski.

CONCEPTS AND COMMENTS

Using a wider ski will give you more height and stability while learning the wake jump. In general, hot dog slalom skiing maneuvers are easier on a wider ski. This usually means that a top-of-the-line tournament slalom is not best for learning because it has a narrower profile. Most manufacturers' "middle-of-the-line" slaloms have the wider profile and still provide excellent cutting and turning performance.

The key to performing a good jump is to properly time the pop, and a hard cut is no substitute for good timing. So don't start those harder cuts at the wake until you have the timing down.

Incidentally, wake jumps are among the few tricks where it's not necessary to limit your number of attempts per set. Jump just until you begin to feel tired. On the other hand, never ski if you feel overtired or fatigued, because this usually causes unnecessary injury.

BOAT DRIVING TIP

While the skier is learning this maneuver, drive the boat two to four mph slower than normal slalom speed.

WATERSPORTS

DOUBLE WAKE JUMP

PHOTO ONE

To do the double wake jump, begin your cut from approximately 20 feet outside the wake. Make an aggressive cut by setting the ski on edge, keep your arms slightly bent, and keep your head and shoulders up. You'll want to generate more speed toward the wake since the goal is to clear the second wake in midair.

PHOTO TWO

About 10 feet from the wake, ease up on your edging and flatten the ski out. It's critical to bend your knees as much as you can in order to attain maximum height. Pop straight up by extending your legs fully as the midsection of the ski reaches the crest of the wake. Keep your arms close to your body and keep your head level.

PHOTO THREE

Hold the same position in the air that you do when performing the single wake jump. To really impress the crowd, you might also want to bring your knees up toward your body to make it look as though you're jumping higher! Don't look down at the water while in the air.

PHOTO FOUR

The landing for the double wake jump is the same as for a single wake jump, except that the shock is much greater. Be ready to absorb the shock by bending your knees as you land. Also, keep skiing in the direction you have been jumping as you land by keeping your shoulders turned slightly away from the boat. Do not immediately try to aim your ski toward the boat as you land.

TROUBLESHOOTING

Problem: Landing off-balance.

Solution: This generally happens when you don't pop straight up. Don't pop off to the side. To do this, make sure the ski is not on edge when you hit the wake.

Problem: Losing control after a good landing.

Solution: This is caused by turning the ski and/or your body in toward the boat too soon. Keep your angle away from the boat both in the air and while you're landing. In

other words, ski away in the same direction that you're jumping.

CONCEPTS AND COMMENTS

Try the double wake jump only after you feel you have the timing down for the pop on the single wake jump. Remember that more aggressive wake cuts translate into more height and distance but can also mean harder falls. Also, the timing of the pop is more difficult because the faster speeds you generate by making an aggressive cut give you less time to push with your legs. To compensate for this, make a quick and more forceful pop.

BOAT DRIVING TIP

When driving for the skier's first few sets of wake jumping, slow the boat down two to four mph below normal slalom skiing speed. As the skier progresses, speed up to his normal ski speed. At this speed, the distance between the wakes is not as wide and the wake is "harder." This allows the skier to push off the wake better. Large, heavy boats create much bigger wakes and a big wake translates into more height for the skier.

MULE KICK

PHOTO ONE

Approach the wake aggressively as you would for a double wake jump or tip drop, making sure to maintain proper skiing form. Prepare for a strong pop off the wake for maximum height and air time. If you do not get good height off the wake, do not try the mule kick.

PHOTO TWO

It is here that you initiate the mule kick. Start to bend both knees and rotate your legs at the hips to get the ski "crossed up." Do not pull your knees up to your chest, but keep them in a vertical line with your head and chest. The tail of the ski should be coming up toward your elbow.

WATERSPORTS

PHOTO THREE

To get into the final in-air position, continue bending both knees. Concentrate on pulling up on your rear leg, and at the same time, relax your front leg. Note that in this photo, the head stays up and the upper body remains straight, even though the ski is in the full-mule-kick position. It is of extreme importance to maintain proper upper-body position in order to make a good landing. Keep your stomach muscles tight so that you can start to bring the ski back around for the landing.

PHOTO FOUR

Bring the ski back to the landing position by extending both legs. Get the ski pointed in the same direction you are traveling before you land. These two steps must be done aggressively or the ski will not come all the way back to the proper landing position. Bend your knees to absorb the shock when you land.

TROUBLESHOOTING

Problem: Ski tip digs in on landing.
Solution: This happens when you don't get enough height and air time. Work on your double wake jump to improve your pop.

Problem: Can't straighten out the ski.
Solution: You'll have trouble straightening the ski if you hesitate to bring the ski back around for the landing. Aggressively straighten the ski out by imagining that you are kicking something. Remember to keep your stomach muscles tight.

CONCEPTS AND COMMENTS

Warm up for this trick by first doing a few double wake jumps and tip drops. If you feel confident and you're getting good air time, try the mule kick. Before you hit the wake, go through the trick mentally. This will keep you from hesitating in the air. You must really "go for it" on this trick, because it is impossible to do half a mule kick! As you improve, you will be able to hold the in-air position longer.

BOAT DRIVING TIP

The boat driver should maintain a straight course and constant slalom skiing speed.

CHAPTER 5:
THE HIGH-SPEED THRILL
OF KNEEBOARDING

GET ON YOUR KNEES AND RIDE

Welcome to kneeboarding, a fast-growing watersport that'll sweep you off your feet and onto your knees! Kneeboarding is still in its infancy, but the sport is growing very rapidly, both in terms of recreation and competition.

At first, kneeboarding was just a recreational pastime enjoyed by thousands, but after people had been riding kneeboards for years, more and more tricks were developed by folks just out of having fun. Nobody really knew what could be done on a kneeboard, nor did they know its limits.

At first, the kneeboard was used strictly for cutting and jumping. Then, riders began discovering just how easy surface tricks could be on a kneeboard; tricks like surface 360s were tried almost immediately by first-time kneeboarders, then such tricks as wake 360s were attempted.

In 1983, an organization called the American Kneeboard Association, or AKA, was formed. Among other things, the AKA developed kneeboard competitions, which are composed of three events: slalom, tricks, and the flip-out.

During the few short years that the AKA has been in existence, it has grown tremendously. More and more recreational kneeboarders are discovering the AKA and are joining and becoming active in competition. In January of 1988, the AKA became affiliated with the American Water Ski Association (AWSA) and is now a member of the AWSA's sports division. This represents a giant step forward for the sport.

Whether you're a recreational rider or an aspiring competitor, you'll find kneeboarding has a lot to offer in terms of thrills, spills, and thoroughly satisfying fun. Now, get ready to enjoy the sport that's brought an entire nation of water enthusiasts to its knees!

GEARING UP

The first thing you'll need to get started in kneeboarding is, of course, a kneeboard! Most boards consist of a hard plastic shell filled with foam for flotation. The top of the board has a neoprene pad to kneel on and a nylon strap is pulled over the knees to hold the rider onto the board while riding.

There are really only two types of boards: some are designed for tricks and some for slalom or cutting and jumping. This is not to say that you cannot cut and jump on a trick board and vice versa. But a certain board shape works better for

tricks and another works better for slalom.

A trick board needs a lot of rocker, or curvature, in the bottom. Also, the rails, or outside edges, must be thick, and the edge should be rounded. The thick rails provide good flotation for lift when jumping the wake, while the rounded rails make the board more "forgiving."

When kneeboarders say a board is forgiving, they mean that if you don't land a trick just right, you can ride away from it rather than falling, which would generally be the case with less forgiving boards.

What's more, rounded rails don't catch and dig into the water as easily as hard, "sharp" rails do. The rocker in the bottom works in the same way that rounded rails do. The rocker keeps the nose and tail of the board from digging in as easily and allows you to make the board "porpoise," which is great for doing air tricks.

A board that works very well for slalom, cutting, and jumping, on the other hand, will have a relatively flat bottom, with only a slight rocker in the nose of the board. The rails (edges) are hard (sharp), which allows the board to track in a straight line. As a result, the board will cut easier and faster and will hold its edge so that you can cut harder.

Some kneeboards have fins and some don't. They're not good for performing tricks, and are primarily for cutting and jumping. Fins are retractable and are best when used for teaching beginners to cut and perform deepwater starts. The fins hold the board in a straight line so that the rider can concentrate on getting up and strapping in. Once up, the fins allow the rider to make the board cut and turn with very little effort. Once the rider is more familiar with the board and how it works, the fins are no longer needed.

KNEEBOARD SAFETY

Safety is very important in all watersports and kneeboarding is no exception. Always wear a Coast Guard-approved life vest when you are kneeboarding. Small children should not use the knee strap until they have advanced to the point where they are in full control of the board. An overturned board might hold them under water if they are not strong enough to pull the strap loose.

Basically, you can use any ski rope for kneeboarding that's at least 47 feet long. If you want to get a rope that can be used for everything, your best bet is a 75-foot slalom rope with "line-off" loops. This way, you can set the rope at any length you want. The best length for practicing tricks is the 28 off loop on a 75-foot line (47 feet).

BOAT DRIVING TIP

The beginning kneeboarder should use the boat speed suggested by the chart below.

WEIGHT (LBS)	BOAT SPEED (MPH)
40	8
50	10
60	12
70	14
80	16
90	18
100	20

Once you have advanced beyond the beginning stages, a speed of 19 or 20 mph is the best overall speed for kneeboarding. There are no speeds given for people who weigh more than 100 pounds because once you have reached 20 mph, you don't need to go any faster. Generally, 20 mph gives you the best wake for kneeboarding. It's only necessary to go faster than 20 mph when you are performing advanced or ultra-advanced tricks.

If you are running slalom, you may want to use speeds of 22 and 24 mph, but it's not recommended that kneeboarders be pulled at speeds in excess of 24 mph. Don't ever go any faster than you feel comfortable. The speeds given in the chart are based on an average. When you first start learning, use the speed suggested, and if it feels a little fast, drop down an mph or two until you feel comfortable on the board.

BODY POSITION

PHOTO ONE

Kneel on the board, positioning your knees about one or two inches from the front of the black rubber pad. Keep your legs close together. Pull the strap up over your legs and place it on your upper thighs close to your waist.

PHOTO TWO

Pull the strap tight and attach it to the Velcro. Sit up straight and lean back slightly. This is the standard position you'll use each time you strap yourself on a kneeboard.

CONCEPTS AND COMMENTS

Spread your ankles wide enough apart to seat your rear-end between them. This is better than sitting on top of your ankles, as it allows you to sit lower on the board, which is the most stable position.

WATERSPORTS

DEEPWATER START

PHOTO ONE

Fasten the strap in its loosest position and push it to the front of the pad. Lie on your stomach with your elbows on top of the strap, about four to six inches from the front of the pad. Your shoulders should be almost even with the front of the pad and your hands should be in the palms-down position on the rope handle.

PHOTO TWO

Signal the driver to "hit it" and use your elbows and stomach as a tripod to balance. Remain lying down until the board begins to plane off.

PHOTO THREE

As the kneeboard begins planing, simultaneously slide both knees onto the pad. Keeping your weight on your forearms, slide or crawl on your knees until they reach your elbows.

PHOTO FOUR

Once in the kneeling position, sit up straight on the board and straighten your arms. Release the handle with one hand and pull the strap over your legs. Inch your knees forward one at a time until they are about one to two inches from the front of the pad.

Face the boat at all times. Position the strap on your upper thighs near your waist, pull it tight, and press down on the Velcro to fasten it. Grab the handle with both hands.

TROUBLESHOOTING

Problem: Falling to the side.
Solution: Generally the result of placing too much pressure on one knee. Slide both knees forward to a kneeling position. Once you get your knees on the pad, you can walk them forward until they reach your elbows. Don't try to bring one knee all the way forward and then the other. This will shift too much weight to one side of the board and may cause you to fall to that side.

Problem: Falling forward over the front of the board after leaning too far forward.

Solution: When sliding your knees forward, keep all your weight on your forearms and elbows. Once your knees are up to your elbows, sit your rear-end down on your ankles. Then sit up straight and lean slightly toward the tail of the board to keep your weight distributed more toward the board's tail. When pulling the strap over your legs, keep your arms straight and centered and remain facing the boat. Don't lean forward.

Problem: Strap slides back when you get up on the board.

Solution: Set the strap in its loosest position before you start. Then push it all the way forward and place both of your elbows on it. This will keep the water from pushing the strap back so that you avoid sitting on it when you get up.

CONCEPTS AND COMMENTS

Practice the deepwater start on land first. Ask a friend to hold the rope and pull on it constantly and evenly while you are trying to get up. This will simulate the boat's pull. Go completely through the steps as if you were in the water.

BOAT DRIVING TIP

Once the kneeboarder is ready, bump the throttle in and out of gear until the rope is slack-free. Slowly accelerate until you see the kneeboard plane, which should be at about 14 mph. Hold your speed until the kneeboarder is up and strapped in securely.

Now you can accelerate up to the speed recommended by the weight/size chart at the beginning of the chapter.

BEACH START

PHOTO ONE

Place the kneeboard near the water's edge. Strap yourself onto the board securely and grab the ski rope handle in the palms-down grip.

PHOTO TWO

When you feel the rope become taut, lean back hard. Keep your arms straight, and as the board enters the water, try to pull your knees to your chest. The front of the board will submerge until the rest of it enters the water.

PHOTO THREE

Continue leaning back and pulling your knees toward your chest. When the board completely enters the water, the front of the board will rise up out of the water. When this happens, you can stop pulling your knees to your chest. Now sit up straight on the board with your arms straight.

TROUBLESHOOTING

Problem: Board "submarines" and doesn't surface.

Solution: You've failed to raise the front of the board as you enter the water. Lean back hard as the board enters the water. Pull your knees hard toward your chest until the front of the board rises out of the water. (This is similar to doing a sit-up, but rather than pulling your chest to your knees, you're trying to pull your knees to your chest. You don't actually pull them all the way to your chest; instead, just pull them up far enough to raise the front of the board.)

Problem: Board starts to porpoise (bounce) because there's too much weight on the tail of the board.

Solution: After the board surfaces completely, shift your weight forward until you are sitting straight up. Then you can lean back just slightly to keep the front of the board a little higher than the tail.

Problem: Boat pulls you over the front of the board or pulls the handle out of your hand because there's slack in the rope.

Solution: Keep your arms straight and lean back hard when the boat pulls you off the beach. If you lean forward or pull the handle in toward your body, you risk putting slack in the rope.

CONCEPTS AND COMMENTS

Make sure that the kneeboard is facing the same direction as the boat before signaling that you are ready to go. If you don't face the same direction, you risk the possibility of the boat's pulling you onto your side.

BOAT DRIVING TIP

Once the kneeboarder is ready to go, bump the throttle in and out of gear until the rope is free of slack. Slowly pull the kneeboard off the beach until you see the front of the kneeboard come up.

Accelerate firmly up to the speed recommended by the weight/size chart at the beginning of the chapter.

WATERSPORTS

STEERING AND EDGE CONTROL

PHOTO ONE

Grasp the rope's handle using the overhand grip. Turn the board to the left by rotating your head and upper body to the left. While pulling the handle toward your right hip, shift your weight away from the boat. This raises the leading edge of the board so that it does not dig into the water.

PHOTO TWO

To turn back to the right, rotate your head and upper body to the right while pulling the handle toward your left hip. Shift your weight onto the trailing edge of the board by leaning away from the boat as you turn. The more pressure you put on the trailing edge, the more it will cause you to cut.

TROUBLESHOOTING

Problem: Digging the nose or rail of the board into the water as a result of improper weight distribution.

Solution: It is very important to keep your weight on the trailing edge of the board in order to raise the leading edge out of the water. Lean away from the boat when you turn the board and keep your weight on the trailing edge.

Problem: Falling over backward as a result of leaning too far back.

Solution: Keep your arms slightly bent as you lean away from the boat. Lean only slightly and use the leg that's on the trailing edge of the board for control. For example, if you feel the leading edge begin to catch the water, press harder on the leg that is on the trailing edge of the board. Don't lean back too far, though.

Problem: Sliding sideways instead of cutting.

Solution: When you lean back slightly, to the right for example, you also want to put all your weight onto your right leg. This, combined with pulling the handle toward your left hip and against the boat, is what makes you cut. If you don't put pressure on your right leg, you will just sideslide.

CONCEPTS AND COMMENTS

Practice turning to the right and left, putting more and more pressure on the trailing edge of the board. Remember that you control the pressure by pressing on either your right or left leg. This is the beginning stage of learning to cut.

CUTTING

PHOTO ONE

Staying directly behind the boat, grasp the handle with both hands in the baseball grip. Lean back slightly to the right and keep your arms bent. Pull the handle in toward your left hip and shift your weight to your right leg. This will allow you to cut to the right. To stop cutting, sit up straight and move the handle to the front of your body.

PHOTO TWO

To cut back to the left, lean back slightly to the left and keep your arms bent. Pull the handle in toward your right hip and put pressure on your left leg. This will make you cut to the left. The harder you pull and lean, the faster and the farther you will cut.

TROUBLESHOOTING

Problem: Falling to the side.

Solution: You will fall to the side if you fail to pull on the rope while leaning. Feel yourself pulling against the boat when you start your lean back to the right or left. It's important to sense that resistance when you pull, because that's what allows you to make the cut.

Problem: Porpoising (bouncing) because you've got too much weight on the tail of the board.

Solution: Lean back to the right or left only slightly, and pull with your arms, not with your body, to control how hard you cut. If you lean too far back, the front of the board will bounce (porpoise).

Problem: Sliding sideways on the board rather than cutting.

Solution: You'll slide sideways if you fail to put pressure on either your right or left leg, depending on which direction you're cutting. When you lean back slightly, for example to the right, you must also put all your weight onto your right leg. It is this action, coupled with bringing the handle toward your left hip and pulling against the boat, that makes you cut. If you don't put pressure on your right leg, you'll just do a sideslide.

CONCEPTS AND COMMENTS

Practice cutting back and forth over and over. Try applying more pressure on your legs and pulling harder with your arms as you get more comfortable. Also practice making a smooth turn as you cut back from right to left and from left to right. This will give you a strong foundation for learning slalom turns.

SIDESLIDE

PHOTO ONE

Riding directly behind the boat, position your hands palms-down on the handle.

PHOTO TWO

Rotate your head and upper body to the left while shifting your weight onto your left leg and leaning away from the boat. This will raise the right rail of the board. Pull the ski rope handle in to your right hip and hold it there.

TROUBLESHOOTING

Problem: Digging the rail of the board in because your weight is not distributed correctly.

Solution: Make sure that all your weight is on the trailing edge of the board. This raises the leading edge of the board out of the water. Remember to hold the handle to your right hip so that the board slides perpendicular to the boat.

CONCEPTS AND COMMENTS

Stay directly behind the boat when learning how to sideslide. Keep your center of gravity over the middle of the board by holding your body upright, keeping your head up, and keeping your eyes on the horizon. This will allow you to sideslide in a straight line without drifting outside the wake.

WATERSPORTS

FRONT-TO-BACK 180, HAND-TO-HAND

PHOTO ONE

Using the palms-down grip on the handle, keep your body upright and your eyes on the horizon.

PHOTO TWO

Rotate your head and upper body to the left while releasing the handle with your left hand. Keep your eyes on the horizon and pull the handle in to your lower back as you rotate.

PHOTOS THREE AND FOUR

Lean forward slightly to shift your weight onto the nose of the board. As you reach the 180-degree position, reach behind your back with your left hand and grab the handle.

TROUBLESHOOTING

Problem: Digging the tail of the board in because your weight is shifted too far back.
Solution: You must shift your weight from the tail of the kneeboard to its nose by leaning slightly over the nose as you rotate 180 degrees. This will raise the tail of the board out of the water. Remember to keep your eyes on the horizon.

Problem: Missing the handle in the back position.
Solution: Be sure to keep the handle in close to your body as you rotate. As you reach the 180-degree position, pull the handle in to your lower back. This will provide your free hand easy access to the handle.

CONCEPTS AND COMMENTS

A problem commonly encountered when riding backward on a kneeboard is bouncing, or "porpoising," which is caused by shifting too much weight over the nose of the board. Once you have turned backward, shift your weight toward the tail of the board until the bouncing stops. Keeping your head up and your eyes on the horizon also helps to stop porpoising.

FRONT-TO-FRONT 360

PHOTO ONE

Using the palms-down grip on the handle, pull it in toward your right hip as you rotate your head and upper body to the left. Release the handle with your left hand and keep your eyes on the horizon.

PHOTO TWO

As you rotate to the 180-degree position, move the handle in close to your lower back. Lean forward slightly to shift your weight from the tail to the nose of the board. Grab the handle with your left hand.

PHOTO THREE

Keeping your head up and your eyes on the horizon, continue your rotation to the left. Release the handle with your right hand and keep it in close to your body as you continue around.

PHOTO FOUR

Lean back slightly to shift the weight from the nose of the kneeboard to the tail. As you reach the 360-degree position, keep the handle in close to your stomach and grab the handle with your right hand.

TROUBLESHOOTING

Problem: Digging the tail or side rail because your weight is distributed incorrectly.

Solution: As you start to rotate to the left, slowly shift your weight from the tail of the board to the nose by leaning forward slightly. This will raise the tail of the board as you reach the 180-degree position. Don't forget to keep your head up and your eyes on the horizon. As you pass the 180-degree position, shift your weight from the nose of the board back to the tail by leaning back slightly. This

will raise the nose of the board as you complete the 360-degree rotation.

Problem: Missing the handle on the hand change.

Solution: Pull the handle in hard to your right hip as you rotate your head and upper body to the left. Keep the handle in close to your waist as you rotate to the 180-degree position. As you reach the 180-degree position, pull the handle in close to your lower back. This will make it easy for your left hand to grab the handle.

CONCEPTS AND COMMENTS

Keeping the handle in close to your waist is very important when performing tricks that require you to rotate on a vertical axis because it provides your free hand with easy access to the handle when you make the hand change. Always bring the handle to the same place at your lower back every time you perform this maneuver. This way, you will always know where to put your free hand when making the exchange.

WAKE JUMP

PHOTO ONE

Holding the handle in the baseball grip, make a strong cut toward the wake. As you approach the wake, target the spot you want to hit and head straight for it.

PHOTO TWO

Just before hitting the wake, stop cutting by leveling your board out and shifting your weight toward the boat. Lean back slightly as the front of the board hits the wake. Maintain a firm pull against the boat and keep the handle in close to your waist as the board begins rising into the air.

PHOTO THREE

Once you're in the air, keep the front of the board slightly higher than the tail by pulling your knees toward your chest. Your body should be upright, just as if you had a book balanced on your head. Continue to pull on the handle evenly while you're in the air.

PHOTO FOUR

Sight your landing on the down side of the wake as you keep the nose of the board up. Prepare for a slight bounce when you land by keeping the handle in close to your waist. (NOTE: The objective is to clear the crest of the opposite wake before you land.)

TROUBLESHOOTING

Problem: Nose-diving because your weight is too far forward on the take-off.

Solution: As the front of the board hits the wake, lean back slightly rather than maintaining a perfectly upright body position. Keep the handle in close to your body and prepare for the boat to pull against you as you clear the crest of the wake. Pull as hard against the boat as it's pulling you as you rise off the wake. If you don't, the boat will pull you forward.

Problem: Falling forward after the landing because your weight wasn't shifted back.

Solution: When you hit the water on the landing, you will bounce a little. Keep your weight back and the handle in close to your body on the landing. When you bounce, continue to lean back and away from the boat. The boat will try to pull you forward as you bounce, so be prepared to pull strongly against the boat.

Problem: Not clearing the entire wake because you're traveling too slowly.

Solution: There are a couple of ways to solve this problem. One is to pull harder against the boat on your cut, so that you accelerate more quickly to the wake. Another is to make a wider cut to the outside of the wake before turning to make your cut toward the wake. This will give you more time to pick up speed before hitting the wake.

CONCEPTS AND COMMENTS

Your ultimate objective when jumping the wake is to land just past the crest of the opposite wake. It's important to aim for the down side of the opposite wake because it acts as a ramp and lets you down smoothly. You won't bounce at all if you land on that down ramp. So when you jump, practice landing on the down ramp every time.

To do this, you must control your speed once you're in the air by pulling the handle into your waist to increase your speed or by extending your arms to decrease your speed. Controlling your speed in the air is the key to fine-tuning the landing of your wake jump. Once in the air, spot your landing just past the crest of the wake. Halfway through the jump, check to see if you're traveling too quickly or too slowly. Compensate accordingly so that you land just past the crest of the wake.

CHAPTER 6:
SKIBOARDING:
THE LATEST WATER CRAZE

SURFING AND SKIING ALL ROLLED INTO ONE

Just three short years ago, almost no one had ever heard of skiboarding. Now, however, skiboarding has truly become another of the world's most popular watersports. Why? Because riding a skiboard is a blast!

Over the years, skiboarding has grown by leaps and bounds and skiboards are now sold nationwide as well as internationally. It is sure to become the family sport of the '90s.

Skiboarding is a high-performance alternative to water skiing, surfing, and kneeboarding. If you enjoy both water skiing and surfing, then you'll love skiboarding because it combines the best of both worlds and offers a fun change of pace. Water skiers who are tired of just turning left and right will find that water skiboarding allows them to experience freeform excitement. And surfers who are tired of fighting the crowds on minuscule waves will find that skiboarding gives them a consistent wave all to themselves — right behind their ski boats! But the best part is, you don't have to know how to ski or to surf to enjoy it!

A skiboard can be ridden behind boats with as little as 20 horsepower, behind tournament ski boats, or behind big 60-foot cabin cruisers. The towrope length can be as short as 15 feet or as long as 60 feet. The boat speed can be as low as 10 mph or as high as 40 mph. The faster you go, the more skiboarding resembles water skiing; the slower you go, the more it resembles surfing. As you can see, the possibilities are limitless and each combination translates into a slightly different thrill. The skiboard's versatility has certainly contributed to its rise in popularity.

This chapter is designed to make the novice skiboarder's first try a little easier and to outline a few basic maneuvers. Skiboarding is truly tons of fun for everyone from six to 60 — so get out on the water and ride!

GEARING UP

Skiboarding is such a new sport that it often goes by other names — surf skiing, for instance. But whatever you call it, it's a world of fun.

Skiboards are usually constructed of super-durable, cross-linked polyethylene and filled with polyurethane foam. This combination results in a lightweight, long-lasting board that is virtually ding-proof.

All skiboards have footstraps that adjust for different foot sizes. They're adaptable to riders who place their right feet forward or to those who put their left feet forward on the board.

Most skiboards have fins that function as an integral component of the board. They play a crucial role in the board's performance, especially in slalom skiboarding, but they can easily be removed for performing 360-degree surface turns and other maneuvers. The bottom designs of the boards vary depending on the complexity of the maneuvers the boards will be used for.

Generally speaking, there's a skiboard for people of all weights, ages, sizes, and ability levels. Be sure to pick the board that is best for you!

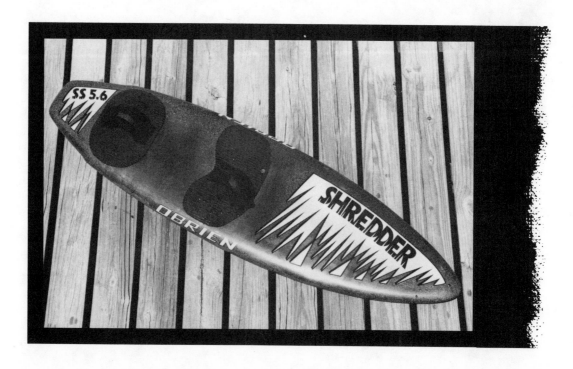

SAFETY IN SKIBOARDING

As in all sporting activities, safety in skiboarding is very important. Always use good common sense when on the water and always — but *always* — wear a snug-fitting Coast Guard-approved life vest. Four-buckle vests are best because they provide better flotation and protection. You'll get a better grip on the rope if you wear gloves, and your hands will be much more comfortable. It's also recommended that you get a good wetsuit or drysuit because it will allow you to extend your skiboarding season and keep you toasty during those early-morning sessions. Also, progress at your own rate when learning new maneuvers. Don't rush yourself.

To learn all the various maneuvers you can perform on your skiboard, it's as important to have a good rope as it is to put gas in your ski boat! Get a rope that's 75 feet long (for slalom skiboarding) and has multiple "line-off" loops. This way, you can easily change rope lengths for various tricks. A braided rope is easier to grab when doing wraparound tricks, and it's important to use a single floating handle with a comfortable grip.

Once you've got your equipment together, just gather your wits about you and get ready for the ride of your life!

BOATS AND BOAT DRIVING

Since skiboards are so versatile, you can have fun on your board behind just about any boat, from a 25-horsepower rubber dinghy to a 60-foot yacht. However, the ease with which a boat can be driven and the size and shape of its wake are very important considerations when you want to advance to new tricks.

The best all-around skiboarding wake is one that is well defined, has a nice gradual slope, and is about 12 inches high. This wake configuration will provide a good platform for aerials and a nice smooth surface on which to turn when doing off-the-wake maneuvers, so look for a boat with these characteristics when you start learning tricks.

It should be obvious even to the novice that the boat driver will play an important role in the skiboarding experience, since a good boat driver will help you learn new tricks faster and more easily. A slightly different technique is needed when pulling a skiboarder than when pulling a water skier or kneeboarder. For starters, because the skiboard has such a large surface area, it is not necessary to use a lot of power on take-off. Generally speaking, if you communicate well with the driver, you will have a better time on your board.

BASIC BODY POSITION

The body position used when skiboarding is the comfortable sideways stance. This versatile stance opens up the doors to maneuvers that are utterly unique to skiboarding; they can't be done on water skis or surfboards. However, the sideways stance is the same one used when surfing, skateboarding, windsurfing, or snowboarding.

If you've ever participated in any one of these activities before, you'll immediately appreciate the natural ease of the sideways stance. On the other hand, if you've never used the sideways stance before, you might find it a bit odd when you first try it.

The most important thing to remember is that a skiboard is not a ski. The most common mistake water skiers make when learning to skiboard is that they face the boat too much. When you do this and try to turn a skiboard as you would a water ski, it becomes difficult to turn and extremely hard to maneuver. Simply *stand sideways*. It's easy, it's fun, and *it works*.

To properly turn and control your skiboard, you must use heel-to-toe pressure. Simply put, this means that when you push down with your toes, the board will go in the direction your toes are pointing; when you push down with your heels, you'll go in the direction your heels are pointing. It's just that simple!

Here are a few other pointers to remember when skiboarding: First, always keep your legs bent. Bending your knees will increase your flexibility and enhance your maneuverability, and is much more comfortable than skiboarding with straight legs. Next, keep your back straight and your hips forward. If you bend forward at the waist, you will probably fall or get pulled forward and go sailing off the board. Last, keep your arms straight. Bending your arms will cause you to lose your balance.

WHICH FOOT FIRST?

Generally speaking, you'll want to skiboard with your right foot forward if you slalom that way, or with your left foot forward if the reverse is true. If you don't ski, just follow the steps in Chapter 3 on slalom skiing to determine which foot to place forward. Just about everyone will place his left foot forward.

FRONTSIDE VERSUS BACKSIDE

There are several terms that are unique to skiboarding. Since this is a new and rapidly-evolving sport, new terminology is constantly being coined. When new and innovative maneuvers are created, new words come along to describe them.

To begin with, it is important that you learn to distinguish between frontside and backside. The sideways stance creates a huge difference between frontside and backside riding. Some maneuvers are much easier to do frontside and some are easier to do the opposite way.

Basically, when you are facing the wake at the start of a trick, the maneuver that you do will be a *frontside* maneuver. Let's say, for example, that you skiboard with your right foot forward, you are on the right side of the wake, and you just laid out a nice, carving slalom turn. You just did a *frontside* slalom turn.

Now, you're heading fast toward the wake and you jump both wakes and get "big air." When you started your jump you were facing the wake, so that was *frontside* air. Now, you're just on the left side of the wake and you're facing away from it. You quickly go for a few off-the-wakes. Were they frontside or backside? That's right, you were facing *away* from the wake, so you did a *backside* off-the-wake.

When you're behind the wake (in between the wakes), and you turn in the same direction that your toes are pointing, that's a frontside turn because you're facing the way that you turned. The reverse is true for backside turns. Got it? Good.

It's a good idea to stand on the board on dry land first and to practice using the sideways stance. Once you've got the basic body position down, you know which foot to put forward, and you fully understand the difference between frontside and backside maneuvers, you are ready to hit the water.

SIDEWAYS DEEPWATER START

PHOTO ONE

Place the board between yourself and the boat and put your feet in the straps. The straps are not meant to be super tight, like water ski bindings, but should be used as a guide. You will notice that the board is very buoyant. Don't try to sink it. Just let it float on top of the water and control it with your feet.

PHOTO TWO

Grab the handle with both hands, using either the baseball grip or the palms-down grip. Put your hands over the board. Keep your arms straight and between your legs. Keep your legs bent a great deal with your knees actually touching your vest. Face the boat. Now you're ready.

WATERSPORTS

PHOTO THREE

As the driver puts the boat in forward gear, push down with your back foot, twisting the board so that its nose faces the boat. Keep your legs bent and your arms straight. The board should be at a 65-degree angle to the water. Keep the board in front of you and use the pressure of the water to help control it. Keep the nose of the board out of the water.

PHOTO FOUR

As the driver begins to accelerate, use the pressure on the board to help you get up. Once the board is turned properly, it will plane effortlessly. Skiboards are so buoyant that they will plane at speeds as slow as 12 mph. Push your hips forward and keep your back straight. About 60 percent of your weight should be on your back foot and 40 percent should be on your front foot. Congratulations: you are now skiboarding!

TROUBLESHOOTING

Problem: Plowing water and having the rope jerked away.

Solution: Twist the board sooner. A skiboard's wide surface area makes it plane easily once it's in the proper position. As soon as the driver starts to move forward, move the board in a 65-degree angle to the water.

Problem: Getting pulled forward.

Solution: You're probably bending at the waist. The easiest way to remember not to break at the waist is to push your hips forward. If you bend at the waist, you lose your balance and the boat will pull you forward.

Problem: Falling to the side.

Solution: Nine times out of 10, the rider falls to the side because his legs are too straight. By keeping your legs bent as much as possible, you have a lower center of gravity and will not fall to the side. Keeping your legs bent also helps to hold the board underneath you.

CONCEPTS AND COMMENTS

The sideways deepwater start is the most common starting method for skiboarders. It is easy to do and most people can get it within a few tries. Also, it's a lot like riding a bicycle. After you get up this way once, you will get up every time thereafter. It's actually easier than starting on a slalom ski, but it is different. If you follow these simple steps, you'll get up with ease.

BOAT DRIVING TIP

Once you see that the rider is ready to go, take the slack out of the rope by idling forward slowly. As soon as the rider tells you to hit it, put the boat in forward gear and start steadily but slowly increasing speed. When you see that the board has been turned at a 65-degree angle to the water, accelerate faster. Once the rider is up, maintain about a speed of 18 to 20 mph unless otherwise indicated by the rider.

WATERSPORTS

FRONTSIDE STEERING
WAKE CROSSING

PHOTO ONE

Face outside the wake, grasping the handle in the baseball grip with your arms slightly bent. Push down on your toes and bend your legs to keep your weight evenly distributed over the board. Since skiboards are extremely responsive, a little pressure with your toes is all it takes.

PHOTO TWO

As you approach the wake, bend your legs a little more to absorb the shock. Keep leaning back slightly and keep the board on its rail and at a good angle to the wake.

PHOTO THREE

Now that you're over the first wake, prepare to cross the second one by keeping your knees bent slightly and keep the board on its rail and at a good angle to the wake.

PHOTO FOUR

As you drop off the wake, you'll notice that your back is now toward the boat. Keep the rope against your forward hip and continue to apply pressure on the board with your toes.

TROUBLESHOOTING

Problem: Falling to the side when crossing the wake.

Solution: Remember, the wake is your friend when skiboarding, but if you try to go over it too slowly, it can knock you off-balance. Keep your legs bent and you'll make it every time.

CONCEPTS AND COMMENTS

Once you're comfortable standing on the board, it's time to start turning and to begin to explore the possibilities of your skiboard. It is very important to learn both frontside and backside steering properly because correct turning and wake crossing will make it easy for you to progress quickly to more advanced tricks.

BOAT DRIVING TIP

Keep the boat's speed constant at about 18 mph. Sudden turns or changes in speed may throw the rider off-balance.

BACKSIDE STEERING
WAKE CROSSING

PHOTO ONE

Start outside the wake with your back toward it. Put your weight on your heels and begin turning the board back toward the wake. Keep the handle on your front hip and arch your back slightly.

PHOTO TWO

As you approach the wake, bend your knees slightly more than usual to absorb the shock. Maintain pressure on your heels to hold the board on its rail.

PHOTO THREE

Now that you're over the wake, you'll notice that you're facing the boat as you head toward the opposite wake. Lean back to resist the pull of the boat. Transfer the rope from your hip to your stomach near your navel. Bend your legs slightly more than usual to prepare for the next wake.

PHOTO FOUR

Use your legs as shock absorbers as you cross the wake. If you want to maintain the backside turn, continue to lean away from the boat and increase the pressure on your heels.

TROUBLESHOOTING

Problem: Falling to the side when crossing the wake.
Solution: Remember, if you try to go over the wake too slowly, it can knock you off-balance. Be sure to keep your legs bent.

CONCEPTS AND COMMENTS

Be sure to spend a lot of time practicing both frontside and backside turning and steering. If you don't get these fundamentals down early, you'll have a hard time progressing to more advanced maneuvers.

BOAT DRIVING TIP

Maintain a constant boat speed of about 18 mph and don't make any sudden turns or changes in speed. If you do, you may throw the rider off-balance.

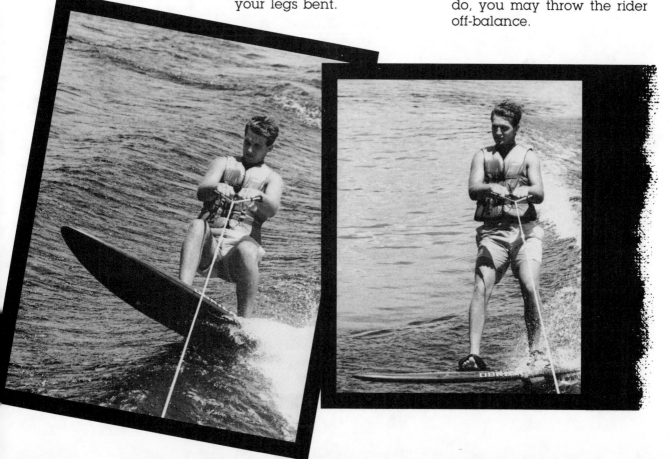

FRONTSIDE SLALOM TURN

PHOTO ONE

Starting inside the wake, head outside and prepare to do a frontside turn by leaning back and putting pressure on the board with your heels. Hold your back straight and keep your knees bent slightly. Use the palms-down grip and hold the rope at your waist. Keep the board on its outside rail.

PHOTO TWO

Move as far away from the wake as possible. As soon as you have reached the turning point, you begin changing rails by transferring all the weight from your heels to the balls of your feet. The board will now be decelerating and it will be on its inside edge.

WATERSPORTS

PHOTO THREE

Now that the board is on its inside edge, you should let go of the handle with your back hand and fully extend your front hand. Straighten your legs and really dig the inside rail of the skiboard into the water for maximum control. For maximum effect, try putting your back hand in the water.

PHOTO FOUR

As you come out of the turn, bend your legs a little and allow the board to flatten out slightly. Grab the handle in the palms-down grip and bring it into your waist. Lean away from the boat.

TROUBLESHOOTING

Problem: Too much slack in the rope.

Solution: You probably didn't fully complete your turn. Concentrate on heading back toward the wake and transferring your weight to the inside rail.

Problem: Nose digs in or the board becomes wobbly.

Solution: Put more pressure on your back foot and extend your legs farther. Remember, a skiboard depends largely on its fins to turn, which are directly under your back foot. Therefore, when you're slaloming, don't let up on your back foot.

CONCEPTS AND COMMENTS

A frontside slalom turn is definitely a thrilling skiboarding maneuver. When you do a good slalom turn, it is a perfect cross between surfing a big Hawaiian wave and skiing on a slalom course.

Practice cutting back and forth many times, and each time you do, turn slightly faster and sharper until you can lay out a nice, aggressive slalom turn that throws up plenty of spray. Like off-the-wake maneuvers, slalom turns are the foundation of many advanced tricks.

BOAT DRIVING TIP

Be sure to get with your skiboarder before he attempts the frontside turn to coordinate your efforts. Drive the boat at a speed of about 18 to 20 mph.

BACKSIDE SLALOM TURN

PHOTO ONE

Starting just outside the wake on your back side, begin turning away from the boat by placing most of your weight on the balls of your feet and angling the skiboard onto its outside rail. Keep your arms in at your waist.

PHOTO TWO

When you want to initiate the turn, throw your head over your leading shoulder and look forward toward the boat. This will help you change the skiboard from its outside rail to its inside rail. Put pressure on your heels and extend your legs.

PHOTO THREE

Let go with your back hand to fully extend your front arm. Arch your back, straighten your legs, and apply pressure to your heels. Hold the board as high on its rail as possible. Use the centrifugal force generated to whip the board back around toward the boat.

PHOTO FOUR

Put both hands back on the rope handle, using the palms-down grip, and pull the handle into your waist. Continue applying pressure to your heels. Keep your hips forward and your back straight to resist the pull of the boat.

TROUBLESHOOTING

Problem: Too much slack in the rope.
Solution: You may not have completed your turn. Be sure to concentrate on heading back toward the wake and transferring your weight to the inside rail.

Problem: Nose digs in or the board wobbles.
Solution: Put more pressure on your back foot and extend your legs farther. Don't let up on your back foot.

CONCEPTS AND COMMENTS

A backside slalom turn, like its frontside counterpart, is thrilling and showy. Practice cutting back and forth over the wake, performing backside turns, until you can turn fast and sharp and kick up plenty of spray. Slalom turns are basic maneuvers that must be mastered before you proceed to advanced tricks and the slalom course.

BOAT DRIVING TIP

Keep an eye on your ski-boarder and maintain a speed of 18 to 20 mph.

FRONTSIDE AIR

PHOTO ONE

Start outside of the wake in the frontside position. Make a frontside slalom turn and begin heading toward the wake. Using the palms-down grip, pull the handle into your waist, push down with the balls of your feet, and keep your legs bent. Try to hit the wake at the sharpest angle possible.

PHOTO TWO

Just before you hit the wake, bend your legs even more to enable yourself to pop higher to get "bigger air." Allow the board to flatten out slightly so that more of its surface hits the water, giving you a better platform for jumping. When you hit the top of the wake, extend your legs and pop straight up off the crest of the wake.

PHOTO THREE

The key to a good jump is to extend your legs completely. Think of the wake as a launching ramp, and as soon as you hit it, jump. While in the air, hold the rope near your waist. Keep your head up and look straight ahead.

PHOTO FOUR

When landing, it is extremely important to bend your knees so that your legs can act as shock absorbers. Lean back slightly and land with about 60 percent of your weight on your back foot. Keep your hips forward and don't bend at the waist.

TROUBLESHOOTING

Problem: Nose lands first and you fall forward.

Solution: This is a painful problem. When the skiboard's nose lands first, the board will stop and your body will keep going directly into the water. This happens when you don't pop straight up and when you put too much weight on your front foot. Bend your front leg more than your back leg when landing to ensure that the tail of the board lands first.

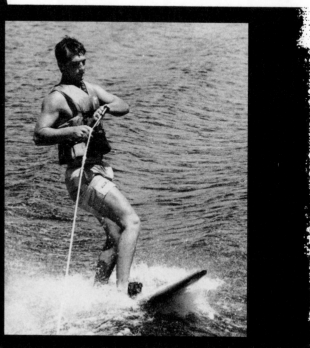

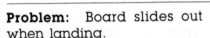
Problem: Board slides out when landing.
Solution: This happens when you try to turn the board too fast after landing. Be sure to continue skiboarding in the same direction you were going while you were airborne. The board's fins need time to catch the water.

Problem: Falling forward while in the air.
Solution: If you look down, you'll fall down. If you are falling forward in the air, it's because you looked down when you were jumping. Look forward and freeze your upper body in the air. There is no need to look down, because you will certainly feel the landing.

Problem: Can't get air.
Solution: There are two key elements to getting good air. The first is timing. If you aren't timing your pop properly, you won't get sufficient altitude off the water. You should time your pop so that you jump just as your front foot hits the wake's crest. Good timing is learned through practice. Go slowly at first and you will have your timing down in no time.

The second problem occurs when jumping up. You can't jump the wake if you don't bend your knees and push off them. Concentrate on compressing your body going into the wake and straightening your legs as you hit the crest.

CONCEPTS AND COMMENTS

Let's face it, getting air is super fun — especially on a skiboard! The sideways stance makes it a lot easier to jump high than the stance used on a regular slalom ski. As you progress, you will begin jumping higher and higher, getting bigger and bigger air. Eventually, you will be able to jump five or six feet off just a 12-inch-high wake.

WATERSPORTS

SURFING THE WAKE

PHOTO ONE

Start outside the wake in the frontside position as far as you can and make a frontside slalom turn. You'll only be about eight feet behind the boat. Make sure to let go with your back hand and hold the handle palms down. Keep your front arm straight, put a little more weight on your back foot, and keep your legs bent. Head back toward the wake.

PHOTO TWO

Just before you hit the wake, start turning the board back away from the wake by transferring your weight to the heels of your feet. Keep your back straight and legs bent. Distribute your weight evenly between your front and back foot, and resist the pull of the boat.

PHOTO THREE

As you bounce off the wake, keep all of your weight on your heels and hold the board on its outside edge. Bend your legs a great deal (so that you're almost in a sitting position). The slow boat speed requires that you make more exaggerated movements. Really snap the turn.

PHOTO FOUR

As you leave the wake, begin straightening your legs slightly, and flatten the board out by transferring more weight to the balls of your feet. Get ready for your next turn by pushing your hips forward and looking back toward the wake.

TROUBLESHOOTING

Problem: Board's nose digs into the wake.

Solution: At these slower speeds, you have to keep more weight on your back legs than usual. Use the back position for the foot-straps and keep your legs bent.

WATERSPORTS

Problem: Board sinks.

Solution: If your board is sinking, the boat is probably going too slowly. The heavier you are, the faster you have to go to get the board to plane. Also, the wider the board you use, the more slowly you can go. The idea in shortline skiboarding is to go just slightly faster than necessary for planing.

Problem: Falling forward.

Solution: If you are falling forward, you are probably breaking forward at the waist. Use your arms and legs to resist the pull of the boat. Push your hips forward and keep your back straight.

CONCEPTS AND COMMENTS

Surfing the wake at this boat speed and rope length is really the core of the sport, because it's the closest that skiboarding comes to real surfing. The rope is shortened so that it's only about five to 10 feet behind the boat. It feels a lot like surfing, but because you don't have to spend time looking for surf, or paddling around waiting for the next wave, you can do dynamic surf-like moves over and over again.

BOAT DRIVING TIP

Keep the boat's speed down to about eight to 14 mph, depending on the maneuvers that the skiboarder does — about the same speed traveled when surfing!

CHAPTER 7:
FEATS ON BARE FEET

BARE YOUR SOLES

Tired of dragging those skis, kneeboards, or surf skis everywhere you go? Are you ready to join the ranks of those who glide on the water using only their own bare feet? Well, it's not as impossible as it looks. With a little determination and practice, you can become a barefooter yourself.

The sport actually got a foothold (pun intended) back in 1947, when both A. G. Hancock and Dick Pope, Jr., successfully performed the maneuver. For years afterward, barefooting was a sport relegated to the ranks of the most daring of show skiers, but by the late '60s and early '70s, more and more "ordinary" skiers began leaving their skis in their wakes.

Today, barefooting is a popular pastime among pros and recreational enthusiasts alike. It's so popular, in fact, that a number of major boat companies produce towboats designed primarily with barefooting in mind. For whatever else it requires — guts, dedication, and tough soles come immediately to mind — a powerful towboat is also needed to generate the speed 'footers need to stand up on their own two feet.

If you feel you've got what it takes to perform feats of daring on your own bare feet, then read on!

WATERSPORTS

GEARING UP

Before you head to the water for a session of bare-footing, you've got to gather together some essential equipment. And first and foremost among your re-quired gear is your towboat.

Although barefooting can take place behind any boat that is able to reach the mini-mum speed for your weight (see chart), there are certain boat and wake characteris-tics that will enhance your performance and help you progress. Let's look at a few of these features.

Acceleration and Top Speed: In general, a boat that pulls an adult slalom skier out of deep water with-out bogging down or strain-ing is sufficient for pulling deepwater barefoot starts. A top-quality barefoot boat should reach top speeds of 44 mph while pulling a bare-footer. Although many skiers may never ski at full throttle, this capability offers addi-tional power, when needed, at slower speeds.

Wake Characteristics: This is the most important feature of a barefoot boat. An opti-mum barefoot wake has a smooth, protected curl, a de-fined crest (not foamy), and a flat and turbulence-free table. Avoid boats with wakes that have rooster tails and excessive prop turbu-lence. A "V" hull usually creates an optimum wake.

Other Features: A center-mounted tow pylon is best. It improves handling and al-lows the barefoot boom to be attached easily. Dual speed-ometers, smooth throttle ac-tion, and rearview mirrors round out the barefoot boat package.

HANDLES AND ROPES

There are many types and variations of barefoot handles, each with its own specific use. All barefoot handles are 15 inches wide, with the exception of the jump handle, which is 12 inches. Quality barefoot handles are equipped with plastic end caps to protect against abrasion.

Another feature to look for is a plastic covered bridle. The plastic covering is a key feature that also protects the skier's body from possible rope burns and abrasions. All handle sections are approximately five feet long and should float or have a float added.

The wake slalom handle is the most practical and versatile in the barefoot line. Its additional length allows for a wider grip and makes the handle easier to regrasp when performing turns. It can be used on the boom or at the end of a long line to perform any barefoot maneuvers except toeholds and jumping. This handle gets its name from the event it is used for at barefoot tournaments.

When choosing a towrope, one piece of advice is always appropriate — use Kevlar, because it provides minimal stretch and maximum durability. A Kevlar line runs down the center of a normal towline, making it a rope inside a rope. It's important to have a no-stretch towrope to prevent you from surging during deepwater starts and to decrease your chances of popping the handle. Low-stretch rope made of polyethylene is a second choice. It is less expensive, but also less durable. Polyethylene rope will, however, get the job done.

BAREFOOT BOOM

Barefoot booms, or training bars, as they are sometimes called, are a great way to practice skiing and barefooting. Proper use of a boom can cut your learning time down greatly, because the boom is a solid bar that can completely support the weight of your body. By hanging directly onto the boom, aspiring and advanced barefooters can avoid many hard falls. Use of the boom also makes coaching easier because the student can be coached from the boat while skiing.

It's recommended that you use a bar constructed of light-weight aluminum, because these bars are fast and easy to assemble, attach to your boat, and disassemble. Make sure all hooks, clamps, and cables are durable and of high quality.

Be detailed and thorough when attaching your boom. Always check to make sure the boom is securely attached to the towboat by means of a tight bracket on the pylon and secure hooks for the front attachment.

Safe boat driving is of the utmost importance when using a boom. The driver should never make sharp turns when a boom is attached. It is dangerous to turn into the boom because it will dip the boom in the water. Always bring the boat to idle before turning around. When returning to pick up a fallen skier, be sure not to pass the boom over his head. Instead, idle by the fallen skier and position the boat so that the skier is beyond the end of the boom. Do not engage in horseplay with a boom, especially when towing a skier.

WATERSPORTS

If possible, use a boom on a larger, more stable boat with a "V" configuration to the hull. Most V-bottomed boats have less side spray and track straighter. One of the drawbacks of specialty ski boats is that they have a severe side spray, and they often cover the boom skier in spray.

BAREFOOT WETSUITS

Barefoot wetsuits are a must for the aspiring 'footer. They make learning a much more pleasant experience because they offer built-in protective padding. In the early days, wetsuits were originally designed for warmth, but modern technology has progressed to the point that many barefoot suits are now a combination life vest and wetsuit. Today's suits provide padding, warmth, and flotation, allowing the barefooter to perform without the exposed edges of a life jacket, which can catch and drag on the water.

Barefoot wetsuits have additional thicknesses of neoprene on the back, chest, and rump for extra impact protection and flotation. These suits, invented in Australia, usually have short legs with cinch straps to prevent water from being forced into the suit during deepwater barefoot starts, tumbleturns, or other maneuvers. They come in long-sleeved, short-sleeved, or sleeveless styles.

Wetsuit shorts are a must under your barefoot suit. They offer added protection and will make gliding on the water easier. There are two types of wetsuit shorts. The first type has legstraps to keep the suit secure and to keep the legs from riding up. This type is great when worn alone, but uncomfortable when worn beneath your suit. The second type is cut slightly shorter in the legs and does not feature straps. This type of short is specifically designed to wear beneath your barefoot suit without being bulky or restrictive.

MISCELLANEOUS GEAR

Male barefooters should wear a protective cup and females should wear wetsuit shorts underneath their barefoot suits for added protection.

BAREFOOT STANCE

Almost all beginning barefooters have a certain misconception about barefooting technique: they think they have to 'foot with their legs extended way out in front of them. The pros don't 'foot that way, and you shouldn't either.

The first aspect of good technique is relaxation. It's important to relax because muscle tension is counterproductive, while relaxation allows you to expend less energy, experience a smoother ride, and concentrate on proper body positioning.

As an example, when a novice is learning to water ski, he will invariably try too hard, constantly pulling and yanking on the handle. The result? His body positioning is poor, he tires quickly, and he takes a lot of hard falls. Remember to relax while you are barefooting. Don't grasp the handle in a death grip, breathe normally, and replace that fearful expression on your face with a smile.

Most barefooters feel they must lean away from the handle, push their legs out in front of their bodies, and anchor their weight on their heels. This may seem like a natural posture, because you're psychologically on the defensive when you first try to grasp the physics of barefooting. In reality, this position is all wrong because weight on your heels creates excessive resistance and can easily cause you to flip over face first.

If you want to minimize falls and maximize performance, it's necessary to place your body in a "seated" position, which is achieved by bringing your legs and feet beneath your upper body, with your feet gliding across the water's surface — gliding decreases resistance. Again, look at a water skier on two skis as an example. If he keeps his weight evenly distributed over the center of his skis, he glides effortlessly across the lake.

Let's apply this same principle to barefooting. The only difference is that the barefooter makes less contact with the surface of the water on his feet than the water skier does using skis, so he requires a faster boat speed. That's the *only* difference.

Are you asking, "Won't I catch my toe?" The answer is, "No!" You don't fall because your toes break the water's surface — this is impossible at barefoot speeds. The real reason you fall unexpectedly is that water pressure begins to sweep your foot or feet beneath your body, past the point where your legs can

support your weight. You then trip forward and fall. This will happen only if your body weight is not properly centered over your feet or if your weight is not distributed equally over your feet.

To eliminate falling and to achieve a position that will optimize your performance, get into the "seated" position; bend your knees, and allow your feet to come beneath you until your shins are vertical to the water. One key point — your legs and feet should always be parallel to each other; never turn your knees inward.

The principle of 'footing with your feet beneath you applies for two-foot positions and also for one-foots and front toeholds. If there is minimal spray in front of your feet, that's a good indicator that you're in the correct position. When your knees are bent with your shins vertical to the water, your weight will be centered over your feet and you will be gliding over the surface, eliminating spray.

The same principles apply to the forward start method as well. Bend your knees and plant your feet flat on the surface (near your seat, not out in front of you). Press down on your feet to stand up (the same way you would when rising from a chair). Don't pull or yank on the handle, relax your upper body, and keep your weight distributed over the center of your feet.

In this new position, a greater area of your foot will make contact with the water's surface. This may feel awkward at first, but concentrate on where the waterline is and practice until this new form of barefooting becomes second nature to you. You'll skim over the lake effortlessly, and you'll start viewing barefooting with enthusiasm!

Here is the proper body position for barefooting:

▲ The feet are slightly ahead of the knees.
▲ The knees are in front of the hips.
▲ The hips are in front of the shoulders.
▲ The head is level with eyes focused on the horizon.
▲ The arms are relaxed with the handle at waist level.
▲ The shoulders are rolled back with the chest out.

While this is the proper position, there are a few subtle techniques to keep in mind. The most important is your foot position or angle in relation to the water. As you know, the waterline should break before the ball of the foot. But should you ride on the inside or outside portion of the foot? The answer is to ski on the inside "edge" of the foot to eliminate throwing spray into your face. Do this by pulling your knees closer together while keeping your feet the same width apart. Also, turn your toes — but not your knees — inward to eliminate spray. This technique is similar to the alpine skier's "snow plow."

WRONG WAY, JOSE!

Although there are many variations on improper body position, these are the most common mistakes novice barefooters make:

▲ Keeping the legs stiff and straight.
▲ Letting the hips trail behind the upper body.
▲ Allowing the upper body to be pulled forward.
▲ Keeping the arms outstretched.
▲ Turning the feet outward, which results in facial spray.

TROUBLESHOOTING

Problem: Body and face are covered in spray.
Solution: Bend your knees and employ the "snow plow" technique previously described.

Problem: Lower back tires quickly.
Solution: Position your hips closer to the handle and in front of your shoulder, and keep your upper body back. This will redistribute the boat's pull from your lower back to your entire upper body.

Problem: Using the baseball grip on the handle.
Solution: Always use the "palms-down" grip when barefooting forward. This provides an even balance and distribution of upper-body strength.

CONCEPTS AND COMMENTS

Think of your feet as small skis that operate on the same principle as full-length skis. You don't normally "tail ride" your water skis, so why put excessive pressure only on your heels? On the other hand, placing too much weight on the front of your water skis will throw your body forward, much like catching a toe. Find the happy medium between these two extremes and you will learn to ski on top of the water with the least resistance.

WATERSPORTS

KNEEBOARD START

PHOTO ONE

Start by lying on the knee-board in the water. Holding the front of the kneeboard, pull your body up and straddle the board. The kneeboard's buoyancy gives it a tendency to pop out of the water like a cork, so combat this by balancing yourself in the center of the board and gripping the sides tightly with your legs. Practice this without a rope or boat — perhaps in a swimming pool. Maintaining your balance on the kneeboard is the most difficult part of the kneeboard start. Learn to balance before moving to the next step.

PHOTO TWO

As the rope tightens, pull the handle into your waist and lean away from the boat.

As the board begins to plane, lean your upper body forward, as you would when doing a sit-up. If the board begins to bounce, place both feet on the nose and slide your butt forward. To do this, grip the nose of the board with your feet and do a "cheek walk" to move forward. Be sure to keep both hands on the handle at all times. Letting go may cause you to turn sideways.

PHOTO THREE

Steer from the center of the wake outside to the curl by shifting your weight in the direction desired.

Once stabilized in the curl, signal the boat driver to accelerate by resting your feet gently on the water's surface. Do this by spreading your feet shoulder-width apart and planting your feet to either side of the board. IMPORTANT: PLACE YOUR FEET FLAT ON THE WATER WITH YOUR TOES CURLED UP. DON'T DIG YOUR HEELS!

Again, do not jab your heels in the water with your feet in front of your body. The objective is to take advantage of as much of the foot's sole as possible without catching a toe. However, under no circumstances should you allow the waterline to break in front of the ball of your foot.

PHOTO FOUR

As the boat approaches barefoot speed, extend your arms and shift your body weight forward. This action will shift all of your body weight over your feet. As you start to rise off the water, you may feel the kneeboard following. This is normal. Eventually, the board will slide behind you.

Be sure to use the proper barefooting position: keep your feet shoulder-width apart, toes curled up, knees bent, handle held at waist level, head level, and eyes focused on the horizon.

TROUBLESHOOTING

Problem: Maintaining balance on the kneeboard.

Solution: Center your weight in the middle of the board and use the tension from the towrope to help compensate for the board's buoyancy. Practice balancing on the board in a lake or swimming pool to familiarize yourself with this technique.

Problem: Kneeboard submerges on take-off.

Solution: Keep the handle in close to your waist, your upper body leaning away from the boat, and your feet close together.

Problem: Uncontrollable bouncing on the kneeboard.

Solution: Caused by placing too much weight on the tail of the board. Some bouncing is normal. Excessive bouncing is solved by sitting up and shifting your body weight forward.

Problem: Falling forward.

Solution: Caused by standing up too early. First wait for the boat to reach barefoot speed, then stand up *slowly* and assume a low, crouched body position until you feel stable.

CONCEPTS AND COMMENTS

The kneeboard start is the easiest method for learning to barefoot. The most difficult portion of this maneuver is maintaining your balance on the board. Don't get discouraged if this takes some practice. The rest of the maneuver is easy!

THE FRONT STEP-OFF

PHOTO ONE

Use a flat-bottomed ski with loose-fitting bindings. Assume a normal slalom position on the ski: keep your head up, your knees bent, and the handle at waist level. Lift your rear foot (also referred to as the "plant foot") from the ski and prepare to rest it gently on the water against the wake's curl.

PHOTO TWO

When placing your foot on the water, be sure to maintain your balance on your "ski leg" by keeping your knee bent with 100 percent of your weight still on the ski. As you begin to plant your foot, place it close to the ski, approximately one foot's length ahead of your ski foot. This is the point where the most common mistake in learning to barefoot is made. The skier either catches a toe or plows and digs with the heel.

As the boat speed increases, push your "plant foot" toward the boat and place it in line with the tow-rope. This technique will help you resist the boat's pull.

PHOTO THREE

Gradually shift more weight to the plant foot as the boat approaches your barefoot speed. The weight transition from the ski to the plant foot should be *slow, steady, and smooth.*

This is a good time to take an inventory of your body position. Ask yourself: "Are my eyes focused on the horizon? Is the handle at waist level? Are my knees bent?" If not, adjust your stance or prepare for a face plant!

PHOTO FOUR

Once 100 percent of your weight is supported by the planted foot, *freeze* your entire body position except for your ski leg. Step away from the ski by lifting your heel off the ski and letting the water pressure pull it away. Gently place your free foot on the water and distribute your weight evenly over both feet. Ride with your feet shoulder-width apart.

TROUBLESHOOTING

Problem: Catching a toe or digging a heel.

Solution: Double-check your boat speed. Be sure that you are skiing fast enough for your weight and size. Make sure the "plant leg" is bent. Exaggerate the knee bend. Check to see that the waterline breaks just behind the ball of the foot.

Problem: Difficulty dropping the ski.

Solution: Be sure the ski binding is loose. One hundred percent of your weight must be supported by the planted foot. Transfer more weight to it!

Problem: Crashing after the step-off.

Solution: Place your free foot on the water *before* shifting weight to it. Too often this step is rushed. Place the free foot *even* with the plant foot, not behind it.

CONCEPTS AND COMMENTS

If you are comfortable on a slalom ski, the step-off will be a simple maneuver. Be sure to familiarize yourself with the step-off procedure on dry land. This is one trick whose dry-land execution is similar to its actual execution on the water.

It's a good idea to break the step-off down in stages and become comfortable with each before stringing them together. For example, stage one is balancing on one leg; stage two is resting your foot on the water; stage three entails shifting your weight to the bare foot; and stage four is stepping away from the ski. Finally, stage five consists of distributing your weight evenly over both feet.

The concept of barefooting is to ski on top of the water. Do this by positioning your foot at an angle that allows the waterline to break up to the ball of your foot, but not in front of it. Conversely, digging your heel will create unnecessary spray and drag. Be aware of and "feel" where the water breaks on your foot.

DEEPWATER START

PHOTO ONE

Start with the handle held into your waist with your toes and/or feet crossed over the rope. Be sure to remove your feet from the rope before releasing the handle. Lie on the water as if you were in bed, with your body kept straight.

PHOTO TWO

When ready to start, signal the boat driver to "Hit it!" As you begin to feel the boat's pull, throw your head back, arch your back, blow air out of your nose, and apply downward pressure on the rope with your feet. Pay particular attention to keeping the handle into your waist and applying downward pressure on the towline. If you don't, your body will break at the waist, submerge, and/or spin like a fishing lure. Decide what you want to be — fish bait or a barefooter!

PHOTO THREE

As your body planes on the surface, take a breath. Don't hold your breath throughout the trick. Some barefooters inhale through their mouths and exhale through the nose, which helps prevent taking in water. Sit forward with your upper body and ride on your butt immediately after planing. Proper timing is critical because it prevents your body from bouncing. Take inventory of your body position: You should be planing on your butt with your legs straight, your feet over the rope, and the handle held into your waist. Get comfortable with this position. There is no need to stand up immediately.

PHOTO FOUR

When ready to stand, shift your weight back so that you ride more on the upper portion of your butt. This will relieve the downward pressure placed on the rope earlier and enable you to lift your feet from the rope. After your feet are lifted from the rope, spread your legs shoulder-width apart and bend your knees *before* you plant your feet on the water and employ the three-point stance described earlier.

TROUBLESHOOTING

Problem: Submerging, plowing, or unable to plane.
Solution: Keep the handle into your waist. Keep your feet on the rope until ready to stand. Keep your body stiff and rigid until planing.

Problem: Rolling side to side once on a plane.
Solution: Caused by not sitting far enough forward. Sit more forward. Dig your elbows in, making them work like training wheels to recover.

Problem: Unable to stand.
Solution: Caused by immediately dropping your feet from the rope to the water. "Lift" your feet from the rope first. When stable, place them in the water.

Problem: Legs are too stiff.
Solution: Bend more at the knees. Extend your arms and shift your upper body forward, as you would when standing up after sitting in a chair.

CONCEPTS AND COMMENTS

The deepwater start is a convenient, time-saving maneuver because it eliminates backtracking to pick up skis and kneeboards. Within a couple of weeks of regular practice, the need for a step-off ski or kneeboard should be totally eliminated. This leaves more time to concentrate on improving your barefooting skills.

CHAPTER 8:

TRICKS ARE FUN
FOR EVERYONE

TRICKS ARE FOR KIDS — AND EVERYONE ELSE!

If you've ever skied on combos, ridden a kneeboard, or even done some snow skiing, you'll find that riding on trick skis is easy, fun, challenging, and the very best way to improve all of your skiing.

To make learning trick skiing easier, it's important to take things one step at a time. Of course, there are individual differences in ability levels — some folks are athletic, others are young, some are timid, and others are downright fearful. No matter what their personality type, however, most skiers learn best when they're not rushed and are given the chance to build their confidence as they progress.

Not every step is necessary for all skiers, but the steps outlined in this chapter should be used as a guide to allow each person to move comfortably at his or her own pace. In this way you'll have fun, build confidence, and develop skills.

Once you get the feel of trick skis, you may find that tricking is your very favorite form of skiing. You're bound to enjoy yourself — because tricks aren't just for kids!

GEARING UP

Trick skis are really nothing like slalom or combo skis. They are shorter, wider, blunt-ended, and have no fin on their undersides. Beginner's trick skis are generally 42 inches by 10 and a half inches. Because they are wide and have an increased surface area, trick skis make it easy to get out of the water without a lot of boat speed and their lack of fins — well, that's where all the fun begins! Beginners' tricks need not be expensive, and should have adjustable bindings so they can help a wide range of skiers learn this important event.

A trick ski that is made for the competitor, on the other hand, ranges in size from 36 inches by eight and a quarter inch to 44 by 11 inches and has fixed bindings. When you reach this level, appropriate selection is based upon height, weight, and age. Competitors use only one trick ski to perform their two 20-second passes.

Trick skis can turn and slide in any direction, so an amazing variety of tricks can be performed, and are generally made of fiberglass. Most models are sold in pairs and come with adjustable bindings, while tournament models are usually sold as single blanks (without bindings) so that the user can mount a custom front binding and a rear toe piece. The rear toe binding on a single trick ski is usually mounted at an angle to center the skier's weight and better control the ski's rotation.

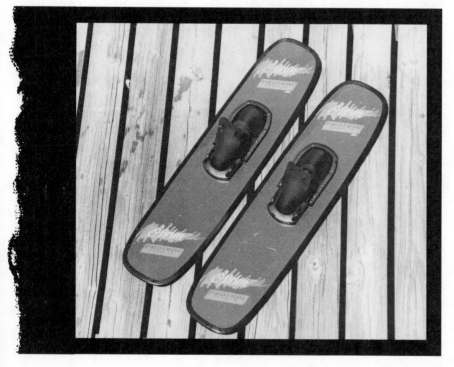

Quality trick skis have beveled top sides that taper to thin, crisp edges at the bottom, permitting the ski to turn easily and keeping the edges from catching. Some trick skis have small grooves on their undersides to aid in tracking when skiing forward or backward. Tip shapes on trick skis vary from round to elliptical to nearly square, but the shape of the tip will not matter all that much to a beginning or intermediate trick skier.

There are two general rules for determining the rope length for tricking. Adults use a 60-foot line, or one loop off the standard 75-foot slalom rope and children use a 47-foot line, or three loops off the slalom rope. Using a shorter rope for young skiers makes it easier to coach them and eliminates droop and "twang" in the rope.

A third, more accurate method for determining rope length is to take the boat up to the approximate speed at which the tricker skis and drop a rope handle into the water. Allow it to drag to a spot in the center of the wake, behind the rooster tail where the table is flat, with a width of 10 to 12 feet between the crests of the wakes. Make a loop in the rope and put it over the pylon or in a trick release. This will allow the tricker to perform in the area of the boat's wakes that's best for tricking.

BOAT DRIVING TIP

Speaking of boats, what's neat about tricks is that you can do them behind almost anything, from a personal watercraft to a small outboard to a beautiful 24-foot family pleasure boat. For learning, most boats are fine. As you rise to the competitive levels, selection of an inboard is critical, because of its characteristically smooth, flat table, and the shape, size, crispness, and slope of the wakes.

The boat speed used for tricks is really quite slow, especially when compared with speeds for slalom and barefooting. For trickers aged six to 12, use the same speed as the tricker's age. Recreational trickers in their teen years should use 12 to 14 mph for learning their skills. Older and larger skiers can accelerate up into the 13- to 15-mph range. Really heavy skiers need 14 to 16 mph to gain maneuverability, and top competition trickers, both male and female, can use between 16 and 21 mph or more.